Mouth of the Donkey

Mouth of the Donkey

Re-imagining Biblical Animals

Laura Duhan-Kaplan

CASCADE *Books* • Eugene, Oregon

MOUTH OF THE DONKEY
Re-imagining Biblical Animals

Cascade Books
An Imprint of Wipf and Stock Publishers
199 W. 8th Ave., Suite 3
Eugene, OR 97401

www.wipfandstock.com

PAPERBACK ISBN: 978-1-7252-5905-8
HARDCOVER ISBN: 978-1-7252-5906-5
EBOOK ISBN: 978-1-7252-5907-2

Cataloguing-in-Publication data:

Names: Kaplan, Laura Duhan, author.

Title: Mouth of the donkey : re-imagining biblical animals / Laura Duhan-Kaplan.

Description: Eugene, OR: Cascade Books, 2021 | Includes bibliographical references.

Identifiers: ISBN 978-1-7252-5905-8 (paperback) | ISBN 978-1-7252-5906-5 (hardcover) | ISBN 978-1-7252-5907-2 (ebook)

Subjects: LCSH: Animals in the Bible | Nature in the Bible | Spiritual life—Judaism | Jewish way of life | Natural history in the Bible | Zoology—Palestine

Classification: BS663 K284 2021 (paperback) | BS663 (ebook)

05/11/21

To Ruthie
Our wild urban mother
May your memory be a blessing

Magic Words

In the very earliest time,
when both people and animals lived on earth,
a person could become an animal if he wanted to
and an animal could become a human being.
Sometimes they were people
and sometimes animals
and there was no difference.
All spoke the same language.
That was the time when words were like magic.
The human mind had mysterious powers.
A word spoken by chance
might have strange consequences.
It would suddenly come alive
and what people wanted to happen could happen—
all you had to do was say it.
Nobody could explain this:
That's the way it was.

Translated and adapted by Edward Field
from Nalungiaq, Netsilisk Inuit Storyteller

Contents

Acknowledgements

THIS BOOK HAS BEEN a ten-year project. Initial ideas came from experiences both solo and shared with Charles Kaplan, Hillary Kaplan, and Eli Kaplan. The ideas blended with my scholarship in philosophy, theology, and spirituality when I was able to share them in classes, sermons, and lectures at Or Shalom Synagogue, Congregation Beth Israel, Highlands United Church, Canadian United Memorial Church and Centre for Peace, Shaughnessy Heights United Church, Ruach Ha'aretz, ALEPH: Alliance for Jewish Renewal, the American Academy of Religion, and The Vancouver School of Theology. At various points, Adele Ritch, Pat Johnson, and Gilah Langner helped me polish the writing. Several snake enthusiasts, who remain anonymous, spoke with me at length about their pets. To help complete the work, the H. R. Macmillan Fund provided a sabbatical research grant. Robin Parry, my editor at Cascade Books, along with the entire staff at Wipf & Stock, extended a calm and helpful hand. Charles, my spouse, discussed experiences, read drafts, and gave his loving support. I thank you all so much.

Laura Duhan-Kaplan
Vancouver, BC
Traditional, ancestral, and unceded territories of the Musqueam, Squamish, and Tsleil-Waututh Peoples

Humans

Imagining Consciousness, Interpreting Bible

WE'RE HIGH ABOVE THE forest on the Skyline Trail in Cape Breton Highlands National Park. The trail's name makes it sound like a route for advanced tundra hikers. But it's actually an easy trail through the woods. A popular, family-friendly walk to a clearing with a spectacular view. The resident moose are quite used to families. The moose lounge in little meadows near the trail and don't seem to mind posing for photos. Most people walk by them respectfully, gawking but talking in whispers. Except, of course, young children. They're pretty loud. And thus, I get to overhear an extraordinary conversation between a thoughtful six-year-old and his mother.

"Mom," the little boy says, "What are deer good for?"

"Well," Mom replies, "They eat leaves and bark in the forest, and . . . um . . . they eat, and that . . . um . . . helps keep the forest healthy. And they . . . um . . . provide food for hunters. And they . . . um . . . live in groups and they're good to each other."

"Do deer know that they're good?"

"No," says Mom. "They don't know they're good. They don't have higher intelligence like human intelligence. They don't have higher judgment like we do. They have a different kind of judgment, like . . . um . . . judgment about when there's danger. It's . . . um . . . like the book of . . . um . . . Genesis says. It says, 'God saw that it was . . . .'"

She waits for her child to fill in the blank.

He says, "Um . . ."

"It was *good*," she says. "Everything God created is *good*."

Technically, I've dedicated this book to my own mom. But I also dedicate it to this mom. Because look how awesome she is! Her child is asking questions with the persistence of a two-year-old. But they're big, metaphysical questions. Yet she takes each question seriously, answering it *exactly* as the child asks it. She considers her answers carefully, pausing to think as she speaks. Clearly she wants to teach about ecosystems, how each plant and animal has an important place. Deer, she believes, have an intelligence well-suited to their way of life. Because they live in families, they even love one another. They don't have "higher" human intelligence—abstract thought and self-awareness—but that doesn't make them unimportant. Because everything God created is good. And she wants her child to share her wonder at the beauty of creation.

And yet. She hasn't a clue what deer know about themselves.[1] But she papers it over with platitudes about human superiority. And when she realizes she is out of her depth, she quotes the Bible. As if it's the ultimate clear answer that resolves all ambiguity. So, this book is a bit of a response to her. A counterpoint, so to speak, with some different views on animal intelligence, God's creation, and the clarity of the Bible. A new trail through the old woods, that, in the words of William J. J. Gordon, "makes the familiar strange and the strange familiar."[2] We won't see moose lounging by this trail. But we will see humans who want to shed their skin, like snake does. A crow who reports to Noah. Sheep who are indistinguishable from our ancestors. Locusts who are very much like the humans they terrorize. Donkeys who lead their riders in spiritual practice. Birds who bring us closer to the image of God. And, finally, cows and bears who understand social justice.

But before we walk the trail, I'll tell you about the roads not taken. And then, I'll lay out some stepping-stones for the journey.

---

1. For a sense of the subjective lives of deer, see Thomas, *The Hidden Life of Deer.*

2. Gordon, *Metaphorical Way of Learning and Knowing*, 4.

If you are an avid reader of books about animals, religion, and spirituality, you will want to know where in the field this one sits. (If you don't, then skip ahead to the next paragraph.) Here, I don't always walk in the wilderness, like author Gerald May does;[3] dwell in a house of science, like Alexandra Horowitz does;[4] see animals primarily as spiritual or psychological symbols, like Ted Andrews[5] and James Hillman do;[6] offer a comprehensive scholarly analysis like Ellen Davis[7] and David Seidenberg[8] do, or catalog every biblical animal, as Henry Baker Tristram does.[9] Instead, I study more in the style of Ken Stone[10] and Debbie Blue,[11] reading selected animal stories carefully and creatively. Lived experience of the animals colors the reading, of course, though I don't pursue it systematically like Elizabeth Marshall Thomas does.[12] But I do bring and also glean philosophical and spiritual views, like David Abram,[13] Annie Dillard,[14] Vicki Hearne,[15] and Robin Wall Kimmerer do.[16] Of course, biblical stories about animals are not written by the animals themselves. Still, I try to listen carefully as the animals speak, and then apply their wisdom. I cannot promise you will find this book wise. But I do promise that you will find some genuinely new interpretations of the Bible's animal stories. So, let's walk together.

3. May, *Wisdom of Wilderness*.

4. Horowitz, *Inside of a Dog*.

5. Andrews, *Animal-Wise*.

6. Hillman, *Animal Presences*.

7. Davis, *Scripture, Culture, and Agriculture*.

8. Seidenberg, *Kabbalah and Ecology*.

9. Tristram, *Natural History of the Bible*.

10. Stone, *Reading the Hebrew Bible with Animal Studies*.

11. Blue, *Consider the Birds*.

12. Thomas, *Hidden Life of Deer; Hidden Life of Dogs; Tribe of Tiger*.

13. Abram, *Spell of the Sensuous; Becoming Animal*.

14. Dillard, *Pilgrim at Tinker Creek*.

15. Hearne, *Adam's Task*.

16. Kimmerer, *Braiding Sweetgrass*.

A Theology of Consciousness

My late mother Ruthie started me on this path. When my brother and I were about ten years old, we wanted a dog. But Mom was dead-set against it. She worried that all the work would fall to her. We disagreed, of course. So, Dad settled the dispute. One morning he secretly took us to a pet store. We came home with a wire-haired fox terrier named Kellie. Mom, of course, fell deeply in love with Kellie. So, for the next forty years, she was never without a dog—or, more precisely, four or five of them. She developed a specialty in helping lost dogs, and ran an informal animal shelter in her tiny urban backyard. No neighbor ever complained, because Mom befriended all of them. She became a strong supporter of animal assistance organizations. She was not in favor of euthanizing pets, and she cared for every dog herself at home until its last breath.

Mom liked to say that dogs have "humanity." Dogs, too, have thoughts, feelings, plans, and hopes. So, we must treat them with respect. And, Mom believed, once you see this, you can't unsee it. You'll realize it's true of all creatures. Mom handed this philosophy down to me. Because it seemed self-evident, I wondered why it wasn't common knowledge. So, as I gradually became a philosopher, I wrestled with the question.

When I was sixteen, I wrote about a logical contradiction.

> *Humans believe they are animals.*
> *Many humans believe animals operate on mindless instinct.*
> *But they don't believe they themselves operate on mindless instinct.*
> *There's a contradiction here.*

But soon I realized there was no contradiction. Only a few false beliefs. A few overgeneralizations. Sometimes creatures, both human and non-human, act on instinct. And sometimes they pause to think things through. But what does that thinking look like?

At university, I learned about Ludwig Wittgenstein's philosophy of language. He said that language reflects a "form of life." We notice things important to our survival. And speak about things important to our shared projects.[17] Wittgenstein was talking about human society and language, but he helped me think about non-humans, too. Other species also focus on what matters to them. Sometimes they notice things humans don't. They think, feel, and communicate about things we don't even know exist. In fact, they have senses we cannot even imagine. For example, humans have a sense of smell. But dogs have a sense of scent. Dog noses receive information that our noses don't. And that information is the basis of all canine knowledge. "For dogs," trainer Vicki Hearne says, "scenting is believing."[18] Of course! A creature's body shapes its needs, its organs of perception, and its knowledge. Creatures experience themselves in ways their bodies allow. The old image of a hierarchy of intelligence with humans at the top now seems odd. We are skilled at our life, and other creatures are skilled at theirs.

Later, in graduate school, I studied phenomenology. That is a fancy word for research into consciousness—how things seem to us. Philosophers understand that human consciousness isn't simple. We've always got a lot going on. For example, we're often seeing, hearing, feeling, thinking, and remembering all at the same time. Each one of those processes puts a different spin on what's happening around us. To sort them out, we have to learn new ways to pay attention to our experience. So we begin with a baby step—"bracketing off" our "natural" attitude.[19] Of course, I was intrigued by these ideas: there's an objective world, but I'm experiencing it six different ways at once! And I'm only one person. What even is going on with other people nearby? Or with other creatures, whose seeing, feeling, and thinking are so different? Could I "bracket off" my experience and try to receive theirs? Well, yes, I could, and in a very practical sense. I could become familiar with their form of life. And try to glimpse the world as they might see it. I could even do it without a biology degree and without leaving the city. Turns out, there's a perfectly respectable name for someone who does

17. Wittgenstein, *Philosophical Investigations*, 19, 23.

18. Hearne, *Adam's Task,* 79–80.

19. Husserl, *Ideas,* 56–58. See also Duhan-Kaplan, "Edmund Husserl."

this: urban naturalist.[20] That's me! I'm not a biologist, just a good neighbor.

So, I did a little research into communication. Observe a creature's form of life, discern its form of communication. That was my working hypothesis, anyway. So, I paid attention to my urban companions. And I bracketed off my everyday view of communication. I didn't look specifically for sound, gesture, or expressions of feeling.[21] Instead, I just watched animals interact. And, bit by bit, I began to learn their languages. Since then, I've conversed with cats by looking at things and then back at the cat. I've given information to wasps and hornets by making gestures. Spoken to crows with vocal clicks and clacks arranged in sentences. (Since I have a limited crow vocabulary, it's a string of nonsense words, but they give me credit for trying.) And, oddest of all, I've befriended flies through telepathy.[22] After all, sight, sound, thought, and movement are all wavelengths on which communication happens. Different creatures favor different wavelengths. A good neighbor pays attention and meets others halfway. It may sound a bit fantastical, but it's really quite basic. In some worldviews, it's simply a way of relating well to your environment.[23]

Eventually, I did translate my experience into theological language. In rabbinic seminary, I studied traditions of Jewish biblical interpretation. Also, I began to learn Kabbalah, Jewish mysticism. Kabbalah is a diverse tradition, but it has some theological basics. God, it teaches, is like an infinite energy.[24] And nothing exists outside of this energy.[25] Our bodies are expressions of it. Our feelings, thoughts, and souls are, too. So is every creature's body, and every

---

20. Haupt, *Crow Planet*, 37–62.

21. Expressions of feeling are noted as core to animal communication by Dean, "Theology, Friendship, and the Human Animal"; Schaefer, *Religious Affects*.

22. As taught in Boone, *Kinship with All Life*, 145–48.

23. See, for example, the Anishnaabek concept of "master of relatedness" in Anderson, *Life Stages of Native Women*, citing McNally, *Honouring Elders*, 51–52.

24. Green, *Ehyeh: Kabbalah for Tomorrow*, Kindle.

25. Margaliot, *Tiquney Hazohar*, 57, 91b.

creature's consciousness. We just all vibrate at a slightly different frequency.[26] So we all express a different facet of divine infinity. Thus, the more we grasp another species' way of thinking, the more we know about God.

Of course, I'm not the first person to imagine that all creatures are, to use biblical language, created in the image of God.[27] Early rabbinic interpreters did the same. As they read Genesis, they asked questions. For example, they were puzzled when God said, "Let us create a human in our own image" (Gen 1:26). To whom, they wondered, was God talking? Who was around to receive God's communication? Why, all of creation so far![28] Light, sky, land, sea, grass, trees, sun, moon, stars, birds, fish, amphibians, and mammals—each a creature in its own right. And each a slightly different reflection of the divine image. This is not the only rabbinic reading of the text, of course, but it is a powerful one. It reminds us that, in the biblical worldview, every creature has its own relationship with God. And thus, when we interpret Bible, animals are not *just* symbols in human morality plays. They are also, sometimes, simply themselves. From my Indigenous colleagues in Canada, I have learned new ways of leaning into these intuitions. We talk often about the creativity of ancient oral cultures; the power of Mother Earth and her protectors; the knowledge involved sustainable living; and the challenge of integrating science with imagination, myth, ritual, and story. All of these, they teach, are also tools for healing from trauma.[29]

Biblical Interpretation

So, by now you've realized that you'll find at least a few unusual interpretations here. But I want to assure you, I found them using strictly traditional methods. I have tried to follow the inquisitive,

26. Rabbi Nachman of Breslov, *Likutey Moharan*, 64:5.

27. See, for example, Seidenberg, *Kabbalah and Ecology*, 47–49; Cherry, *Torah through Time*, "The Creation of Humanity," 40–71.

28. *Bereisheet Rabbah*, 8:3 on Gen 1:26.

29. Aldred and Kaplan, *Spirit of Reconciliation*, 14–15.

imaginative spirit of early rabbinic interpreters. Their style of interpretation is called by the simple name *midrash,* "interpretation." According to James Kugel, early rabbis read the Tanakh, Hebrew Bible, with four assumptions in mind: it is divine, cryptic, flawless, and always relevant.[30] But they understand the assumptions a bit whimsically. Yes, the Bible is divine speech, i.e., the most meaningful speech possible. It's loaded with so much meaning that humans will never fully map it. We study in groups, learn old interpretations, craft new ones—and we still barely scratch the surface. So, of course, the Bible is and always will be cryptic. And, really, it's hardly flawless. The stories, poems, and aphorisms were shared, recorded, edited, and re-edited by fallible human beings. Repetitions, inconsistencies, and puzzles show up everywhere. But instead of seeing problems, early rabbinic readers saw opportunities. And so, at every opportunity, they asked a creative question. Then, they came up with an imaginative answer, grounded in the biblical text. And when you're always engaging that deeply, the text is always relevant.

In another way, too, the early rabbinic interpreters saw the text as always relevant. Each section, they said, is relevant to all the others. Storytelling stops and starts, metaphors recur, scenes hint at one another. Sometimes, the Bible gives information in a non-linear way. So, when we have a question about one chapter, we might find a clue in another one. It does not matter which one comes first in the table of contents; no one knows for sure when they were written or edited. Thus, the rabbis often read the Bible as if nothing is definitively earlier or later.[31] Occasionally they read historically. For example, they saw Moses and Miriam as historical figures, and they made educated guesses about authors of the later books. But, for the most part, they used a literary style of reading, which I follow. Rarely do I draw on historical criticism, i.e., study of the history of the biblical text itself. This is not because I believe God literally wrote the Bible; obviously, human storytellers, writers, and editors shaped the text over time.

30. Kugel, *The Bible As It Was,* 18–23.
31. See, for example, *Tanchuma,* Terumah 8:1.

In medieval times, Kabbalistic teachers created a four-leveled method for interpreting Torah. And, in a way, I use all four of those levels here. I look at *peshat*, plain literal meaning; *derash*, exposition of recurring ethical themes; *remez*, hints to allegorical meanings; and *sod*, secret allusions to God's true nature. And, like all interpreters, I bring background cultural and religious knowledge to my readings.[32] *Peshat* appears when I bring in information about the animals, as I do, for example, in the donkey chapter. Biblical authors wrote about animals they knew. So, if we want to understand them, we need a taste of their background knowledge. *Derash* appears when I make inter-textual allusions, noting connections between words and themes in different books. I assume that motifs recur because they express values important in biblical culture. From there, it is a small step to teach about biblical ethics, as I do, for example, in the locust chapter. *Remez* appears when I articulate a hidden, metaphorical level in the biblical text, as I do in the sheep chapter. And *sod* appears when I draw on Kabbalah to show how human insight reflects divine movement itself, as I do in the eagle chapter. Of course, as biblical scholar Michael Fishbane points out, "we live in multiple life worlds simultaneously,"[33] so I am not always able to clearly separate the four approaches.

When I read with a literary eye, odd patterns and puns catch my eye. So, sometimes my writing here is whimsical. Hebrew Bible is filled with funny, wry observations, and I highlight some of them. But, other times, I'm quite serious. Why, I wonder, did the storyteller use these words? What did they want us to notice about the animals? About ourselves? God? Our ecosystems? What do these details mean in a time of ecological crisis? If we read the Bible for cultural perspective and spiritual guidance, what can we learn? A great deal, it turns out, about hierarchies and webs of life. Interdependence of humans and other animals. Local economies. Waste reduction. Consequences of exploiting land and people. Shifting our consciousness. And, finally, hope.

32. Fishbane, "Ethics and Sacred Attunement," 425–29.
33. Fishbane, "Ethics and Sacred Attunement," 429.

Biblical Ethics

Ecological activism is not a core theme of this book. But I have written it in a time of ecological crisis. You may even be drawn to read about animals in the Bible because of your own ecological worries. So, please know that some of my thoughts about environmental ethics do thread through the book. Because of climate change, human communities are disrupted.[34] Other species are dying off quickly.[35] These problems are caused, in part, by human greed. For example, many companies mine regions for resources and leave without a clean-up plan.[36] They pay fines rather than clean up, lobby legislators to lift environmental regulations, and pour money into discrediting environmental science.[37] In response, activists have issued policy proposals with calls-to-action.[38] So, I won't duplicate or even summarize their ideas here.

But, I do want to note that biblical ethics takes the side of environmentalists. Consistently, biblical narratives and teachers oppose greed. They champion small, sustainable communities. In a few of the chapters here, I rely explicitly on this biblical ethic. As I see it, it is rooted in the community of mutual support described in the book of Leviticus. There, communal health is like a delicate force field. Grief, illness, or crime disturb it. But people can help reset it, with rituals of consolation, healing, and restitution (Lev 1:1—5:26).[39] And with limits on economic inequality (Lev 26:3–46). Some inequality is inevitable, of course, based simply on environmental luck. But the lucky share their wealth with everyone: native, immigrant, male, female, family, strangers, abled and disabled. Landowners hire all kinds of people and pay them promptly, with a living wage. They run a harvest-time

34. Rush, *Rising*.

35. Wilson, *The Creation*, 73–81.

36. Hedges and Sacco, *Days of Destruction*; Korten, *When Corporations Rule*, 59–72.

37. Bakan, *The Corporation*; Lewis, *The Fifth Risk*; Ivins and Dubose, *Bushwhacked*; Oreskes and Conway, *Merchants of Doubt*.

38. Naomi Klein, *This Changes Everything*; Seth Klein, *A Good War*.

39. See also Milgrom, *Leviticus: A Continental Commentary*.

fresh-food bank and pay taxes to support the poorest. Also, they offer interest-free loans because, without them, borrowers fall deeper and deeper into debt.

Along with these consistent ethical practices, Leviticus recommends regular economic and ecosystem resets. Every seventh year, agricultural landowners should let their fields lie fallow. They should forego profit, welcome foraging humans and animals, and let the land rest. Every fiftieth year, creditors should forgive loans, and free indentured servants.[40] Without these resets, Moses says, society's energy field would fail. Social safety nets would be overstressed. People would lose hope in a healthy life. Their anxiety and depression would grow, too. They would blame each other, become paranoid, and invent imaginary enemies. The community would fracture. Unable to unite in self-defence, it would be vulnerable to invasion. People would pray for rescue. But without social action, their prayers would be useless. Finally, after many deaths, their arrogance would be broken. And, together they would find their way back to right living (Lev 25:1–55).

Thus, the Bible insists, there is hope. True, the challenges of human community will never be solved once and for all. But that's why we keep working and learning, thinking and re-thinking. The Tanakh gives us great tools, opening our eyes to different ways of living in the world. And, if we interpret it with it a midrashic eye, it also invites us to critical and creative thinking. So, maybe we can take another look at the moose lounging by the Skyline Trail. Or, rather—since moose don't show up again in this book—at what it means to say, "everything God created is good."

---

40. Morrison, *Gold from the Land,* "Behar: Jubilee—National Reconciliation."

Sheep

Living Well on the Land

AN ANONYMOUS MEDIEVAL JEWISH work of eco-spirituality describes creation as a choir. In it, each animal, plant, and geographic feature sings a different Bible verse. In Hebrew, this book's name is *Perek Shira*. Because this simply means "Chapters of Song," English translators have named it more expressively as "Nature's Song," or "The Song of the Universe."[1] Perhaps *Perek Shira* was inspired by Psalm 148, in which celestial objects, sea monsters, weather patterns, plants, animals, and humans of every social class praise God. But we cannot know for sure the author's intentions, because their name is lost to us. Still, it's fun to speculate.

The Power of Sheep

According to *Perek Shira's* author, sheep chant, "Who is like you among the gods, YHWH? Who is like you, majestic in holiness? Awesome, shining, maker of miracles!" (Exod 15:11).[2] This verse sits at the middle of the Song of the Sea, a formal poem Moses sings after the Israelites cross the Red Sea. In the Song, Moses praises God for vanquishing Pharaoh's army with terrifying power.

---

1. Nathan Slifkin, *Perek Shira: Nature's Song*; Sherman, *Perek Shira: Song of the Universe*.
2. All translations from Hebrew are mine, unless otherwise noted.

Why? Why did the author imagine sheep sing this particular verse? In one commentary, Rabbi Nosson Sherman offers his theory. Sheep are prey, he says. They have no defenses against predators. So, like the Israelites fleeing Egypt, sheep only survive because God is awesome.[3]

However, this cannot be right. It is based on a terribly inaccurate description of sheep. Actually, sheep have many means of defense against predators. For example, their hearing and vision are hyper-acute. Because they use each ear independently, sheep can pinpoint the exact source of a sound. Some breeds can see 300 degrees—almost a complete circle—around their bodies. Sheep also share information with one another through body language. When one wise sheep gestures "Danger!," an entire flock can move in unison. Once, while I was hiking in Scotland's highlands, a center of shepherding culture, a flock leader noticed me. She turned her shoulder ever so slightly. By the time I blinked, the whole group had flown off like a single white cloud. And those are domestic sheep! I have also seen wild sheep walk right up a sheer vertical rockface, where no predator can follow. And there's more. Sheep are not just prey animals. Maybe to a large mammal, a sheep looks like dinner. But to a plant, a sheep looks like a fierce predator. Normally, plants defend themselves with bark, burrs, thorns, and shells. But none of these deter sheep. Sheep will eat an entire fruit tree—bark, shells, and all.

So why, in *Perek Shira*, do well-defended, predatory sheep sing "Who is like you, YHWH, awesome in splendor"? Here is my alternate theory about what the author had in mind. The sheep are simply singing along with Moses at the sea. The Torah states explicitly that sheep are part of the exodus. Pharaoh tells Moses, "Take your sheep and cattle and go!" (Exod 12:32). And soon the voice of the narrator reports that "600,000 adult males . . . and sheep and cows, a great load of livestock" left together (Exod 12:38). Here, as in other stories, the lives of the Israelites are closely entwined with the lives of their sheep.[4]

3. Sherman, *Perek Shira*, 81.
4. See, for example, Fleming, "Living by Livestock in Israel's Exodus."

Sheep or Shepherd?

Just how closely are shepherd and sheep linked in the biblical imagination? Let's look at the story of Jacob, whose spiritual name, Israel, becomes the name of his clan. The story begins with the coming-of-age story of this young herdsman. Jacob and Esau are the twin sons of wealthy shepherds. Jacob, the younger twin, is described in Hebrew as *tam*, perfect (Gen 25:27). He likes the shelter of tents. Esau, the elder, who happens to be unusually hairy, prefers hunting in the great outdoors. Esau and Jacob struggle over the birthright. So, Jacob leaves town to get away from his brother and to find a wife. He meets the shepherd women Rachel and Leah. Rachel has beautiful form and Leah has weak eyes. They live with their father Laban. Jacob tries to marry Rachel, but Laban insists that he marry Leah first. As Jacob matures, he becomes a master sheep breeder. Eventually, he separates from his father-in-law to start his own successful business. He encounters his brother Esau, who is now a wealthy landowner. Jacob is still afraid of his older brother. But he wrestles with his phantom, changes his name to Israel, and reconciles with Esau.

So far, much may be familiar. But here's the new perspective. *Jacob's story is also the coming-of-age story of a young sheep.* Perhaps, millennia ago, the story's audience appreciated this right away. And maybe they even laughed with delight. But, today, we have to decode the story to see it. Some clues are hidden in the characters' Hebrew names. Others are plot points that make subtle reference to shepherding knowledge. So, when I read *Storey's Guide to Raising Sheep,* I figured out how to connect the dots.[5]

One of the dots is the naming story of newborn twins Esau and Jacob. Esau comes out of the womb "red, his whole body like a magnificent hairy (*se'ar*) cloak" (Gen 25:25). So, using a similar sounding word, his parents name him *Esav*—rendered in English as Esau. Jacob comes out with "his hand holding Esau's heel (*akev*)" so his parents name him *Ya'akov*, one who follows at the heel—rendered in English as Jacob. Other characters' names, coupled with

---

5. Simmons and Ekarius, *Storey's Guide to Raising Sheep.*

their personality traits, are important here, too. Thus, in rendering their names, I depart only very slightly, if at all, from their most plain meanings. So, here goes.

Two little sheep are born, named Wooly (Esau) and Follower (Jacob). Follower is a shepherd's dream lamb. He is *tam,* perfectly formed with no physical imperfections. Wooly, however, is born with wool on his face and legs. Shepherds don't really like this condition. This extra wool is coarse, hard to shear, and impossible to sell. Shepherds consider it a plus only if the sheep have to live outdoors most of the time. So that's what Wooly does. He lives most of his life outdoors.

When Follower matures, he sets out on his own, so he can find a mate from a neighboring flock. And so he won't have to compete with Wooly. At a watering hole, Follower meets a small flock of sheep. It includes two females named Ewe (Rachel) and Wild Mama (Leah), and their father, Whitey (Laban). Ewe is *ye-fat toar,* literally, beautifully formed. Like Follower, she was born with what shepherds call "good conformance." Wild Mama has a non-fatal birth defect troubling to shepherds. Her inverted eyelids cause her eyes to tear.

Follower falls instantly in love with Ewe and wants to mate with her. But Whitey, a dominant male, has other ideas. He pushes Follower to have many lambs with Wild Mama. Eventually, Whitey allows Follower to mate with Ewe. As expected, they produce a lamb with perfect conformance (Joseph), who fetches a very high price when he is later sold in Egypt.

Over time, Follower becomes a fully mature ram. He decides he's ready to set out on his own with his flock. But he smells Wooly in the air and his hormones kick in. Even though he hasn't seen Wooly yet, he fights for dominance with a phantom. He feels that he wins. After all these years, he is finally the dominant male of his flock. He lets go of his birth name, Follower. He calls himself Wrestler Prince (Israel).

The sons of Wrestler Prince stay together in a single large flock. But they, too, struggle for dominance and independence. Eventually, the flock migrates to Egypt to graze in the fertile land of Goshen. Egyptians enslave them. But their shepherd Moses leads them to freedom across the Red Sea, pointing the way with his shepherd's staff. Of course, the newly liberated sheep—both human and ovine—sing God's praise.

Living as a Family on the Land

The double meanings woven into the Jacob family story would certainly delight a shepherding audience. But they are not just expressions of literary cleverness. They also remind us of one biblical understanding of ecology. Shared life on the land weaves species into a single resilient web of life. Anthropologist Mary Douglas even says that sheep are part of the Israelite covenant community. Only animals in this community, she says, are considered fit to eat or offer to God.[6] For ten years, I wondered what she meant and now, finally, I have an idea. A few summers ago, I took an Indigenous Studies course called "The Land Is Sacred." The teacher, Ray Aldred, a Cree from the Treaty 8 region in Alberta, Canada, likes to say, "The land is our mother." He often speaks of treaties as ways of "seeking proper relatedness in the land."[7] And he helped me realize: all my life, I have only seen improper relatedness.

Environmental theologian Norman Wirzba clearly describes both kinds of relatedness. Wirzba, also from Alberta, is the son of farmers of European descent. Food, Wirzba says, links us in community. We eat with our friends, families, and religious communities. But the ingredients we cook with often don't come from our communities. Instead, a global food system delivers them. Because more than half the world's population lives in cities, most of us humans don't grow, gather, raise, or hunt our own food. Instead, we buy it in the supermarket. So, we don't know the history of our food. If it's plant-based, then we don't know how it came out of the land, what kind of soil it likes to grow in, which insects pollinate it, or how to protect it through weather changes. If our food is

6. Douglas, *Leviticus as Literature*, 41–65.
7. Aldred and Duhan-Kaplan, *Spirit of Reconciliation*, 10.

animal-based, then we don't know how it lives, adapts to different seasons, or behaves at different times in its life cycle. So, we often eat without any conscious connection to the land.[8]

But a local food system does link us to the land. To survive, we get to know local soil, plants, and animals. We learn how to harvest in a way that keeps the ecosystem stable. Depleting the land is not an option, unless we wish to migrate or starve. So, we structure our community around the ecosystem. We create a division of labor that helps us reap, produce, and preserve. Our whole way of life attunes us to the land. The land, we would then say, births us, feeds us, teaches us, and sustains us. Together, we function as a family on the land. Animals and plants, both wild and cultivated, are part of this family circle of support. Yes, some are food animals who are well-cared for during their lives. All are part of the community that lives well together on the land. In this sense, they are part of a treaty or, in biblical language, a covenant.[9]

Protesting Animal Sacrifice

So that's the view expressed in Genesis: sheep are kin. But, in biblical time, Genesis represents a simple, pastoral past. Once the nation organizes into a federation, the status of sheep changes. In Leviticus, for example, sheep are simply a commodity. Leviticus sets out the system of food offerings for the sanctuary. It's a sliding scale system; people bring what they can afford. Grains, birds, sheep, goats, cattle. Sheep seem to be the middle-class donation of choice.

Some of the donated sheep are eaten. People celebrate happy milestones with a *zevakh shelamim*, party offering, eaten by a joyful host and their guests. Repentant criminals who have compensated their victims also bring an *asham*, guilt offering. This fine, paid in livestock, feeds the priests who work as public servants in the sanctuary.

8. See Wirzba, *Food and Faith*; *The Paradise of God*.

9. Battiste, *Living Treaties*; Miller, *Compact, Contract, Covenant*; Government of Canada, "Peace and Friendship Treaties."

But some of the donated sheep are destroyed for ritual purposes alone. The *khataat*, the psychological purification offering, is cooked in fire, until nothing remains. The animal disappears just as the donor hopes their inner pain will. The *olah*, daily offering, is burned up every morning and evening, connecting earth and heaven with a column of smoke. Leviticus sees these rituals as essential to community health. They help people celebrate, atone, rebalance, pray.[10]

But some of these rituals seem so wasteful! Surely, even in the world of Leviticus, *someone* must have opposed them on ethical or economic grounds. Is such an objection recorded? Yes, I believe it is. Two young priests, Nadab and Abihu, do protest. But their story is told quite delicately. So, to understand what happens, we will copy the style of medieval Jewish commentators. We'll scan nearby passages for clues, and try to fill in the blanks.

It's opening day at the *mishkan*, literally God's local dwelling place, also known as the traveling wilderness tabernacle. The *mishkan* is a kind of community center, funded by donations, and built by local artists. Just a week ago, Aaron and his sons were ordained as priests. Just one day ago, they completed a week-long spiritual retreat. Now, on the eighth day, Aaron's brother Moses gives them detailed instructions for the opening-day ritual. Aaron and his sons seem to follow them carefully. Step by step, Aaron prepares three meat offerings and a grain offering. There's a *khataat* to purify the sanctuary, the inaugural *olah,* and a *shelamim* to get the party started. Together Moses and Aaron bless the people. All of them experience God's glory. Then, a fire flashes forth from God's presence and burns on the altar. Everyone experiences God's glory. They cry out and fall on their faces in prayer (Lev 9).

And then, two of Aaron's sons, Nadab and Abihu, pick up their incense pans. In the pans, they place fire and then incense. They approach the presence of God. *But their offering was not part of Moses' instructions.* Fire flashes forth from God's presence and burns them. Thus, they die in the presence of God. Moses says this

---

10. Milgrom, *Leviticus 1–16;* Duhan-Kaplan, "The Blood of Life."

proves that Nadab and Abihu are intimate with God. But Aaron is stunned into silence (Lev 10:1–3).

What the bleep happened? Why do they die?

Our medieval commentators want to know, too. They accept Moses' view that Nadab and Abihu are full of spiritual zeal and thus, good intentions. So, they infer, something goes wrong with the ritual performance. Later genealogies call it a "strange fire" (Num 3:4; 26:61). But what exactly was strange? Some commentators find answers in what Nadab and Abihu do just before they die. These commentators conclude that the young men take too many safety risks. They should not have put incense directly into the fire.[11] Or they should not have lit their fire at all, but waited for God.[12] As new priests, they should not have strayed from Moses' instructions.[13]

Other commentators find clues in the events just after Nadab and Abihu die. Right away, God gives Aaron a few extra rules to follow at the sanctuary. They're intended, commentators assume, to prevent future accidents. For example, God says, "Don't drink wine or liquor on the job, so you won't die" (Lev 10:8). This shows Nadab and Abihu drank a little too much at the party to be safe around fire.[14]

But these creative readings do not go far enough. And I mean that literally! The commentators take clues only from the nearest verses. But if you read a little farther into the chapter and the story, you see more. And you can draw different conclusions. Like this one, for example:

Nadab and Abihu are opposed to eating animal offerings. So, on opening day, in front of crowds, they stage a symbolic demonstration, offering "a strange fire." For sure, it is not part of the script Moses prepared. Maybe it is a vegan offering of pure incense. And

---

11. Nachmanides on Lev 10:1, in Carasik, *Commentator's Bible,* 61.

12. Rashbam on Lev 10:1, in Leibowitz, *New Studies in Vayikra Leviticus,* 126.

13. Rashi on Lev 10:2, in Carasik, *Commentator's Bible,* 62.

14. Ibn Ezra on Lev 10:9, in Carasik, *Commentators' Bible,* 65. See also Wolak, "Alcohol and the Fate of Nadab and Abihu."

a mistake, a sloppy calculation of ingredient ratios, causes the fire to flare up. Or maybe it is a dramatic act of self-immolation, in which Nadab and Abihu throw themselves on the flames. Moses and Aaron note the acts of protest, but they still enact the system of animal offerings.

Here's how the story continues. After Nadab and Abihu die, Moses reminds Aaron that he must eat the meat offerings. God made this rule, says Moses, and it holds forever. But then Moses finds the meat burned rather than eaten. He gets angry with Aaron's surviving sons. "Why didn't you eat this meat at the sanctuary?" he demands. But Aaron now speaks up. "Given all that happened today," he says, "Do you really think God would like us to eat this?" (Lev 10:12–19). It's possible Aaron means, "My sons died trying to limit the slaughter. I won't dishonor their memory by eating meat in public."

And then God speaks up. Moses and Aaron should talk with the people. Tell them that yes, they can eat meat. But only from animals with split hooves who chew their cud. In other words: sheep, goats, and cows—the very animals preferred for burnt offerings (Lev 11:1–3). Maybe the death of Nadab and Abihu shakes the community. Fellow Israelites begin to worry that an endless stream of burnt offerings is unsafe. They question the need for so many ritual meat meals. So, God reassures them that their diet is just fine.

Finally, some time "after the death of Aaron's two sons" (Lev 16:1), Moses instructs Aaron in a new annual ritual. Aaron will purify the sanctuary, atoning for himself, his family, and all the people. Aaron will bring forward two goats. One will be driven into the wilderness. This will be the "goat of *Azazel*," Aramaic for the "goat that went away." The other, "the goat of YHWH," will be incinerated on the altar. Aaron will use a lottery to decide which is which (Lev 16:8). Luck of the draw will determine the animals' fates.

With this ritual, Aaron acknowledges the two views that tore his family apart. There's the view of his brother Moses, who promotes animal offerings. And the view of his sons Nadab and

Abihu, who protest them. Ultimately, Aaron sides with Moses, and implements his program. But, with this ceremony, Aaron keeps the dissenting voice alive. Yes, some say the animal offerings are wasteful and unfair. For now, that's not the ruling opinion. But one day, economic and ethical culture may change. And then, Nadab and Abihu's philosophy will win the historical lottery.

For now, Leviticus preserves their story in a "counter-tradition," as scholar Ilana Pardes calls it.[15] The Bible represents the mores of a dynamic, diverse group of people. A master story has emerged, but minority voices also peek through the narrative cracks. So do stories of their censorship. I'm sure the story of Nadab and Abihu is a story of protest and censorship. But I'm not yet sure exactly which counter-tradition they represent—though I have a strong opinion.

Maybe Nadab and Abihu are vegetarians who find meat-eating wasteful and cruel. Theirs would not be the only biblical voices suggesting a vegan diet is morally superior. Isaiah, for example, in his oracle of a just and peaceful future, envisions a time when no animal eats another (Isa 11:6–9). The prophet Daniel, raised as a captive courtier in Babylonia, resolves to avoid a rich royal diet. He and his three friends eat vegetables, legumes, and seeds. Thus they grow "more attractive and healthy looking" than the other courtiers-in-training. God gives them "knowledge and intelligence" so that they answer the king's questions "ten times better" than anyone else (Dan 1:21).

Or maybe Nadab and Abihu support farmers over shepherds. So they worry that the system of offerings will enrich shepherds but impoverish farmers. Economic tensions between the two groups do show up in other stories. Sometimes shepherds win the conflict and sometimes farmers do. In the story of Cain and Abel, God prefers the shepherd's animal offering. Cain, the jealous farmer, responds with violence and is punished (Gen 4:1–18). But in the story of rebellious shepherds Dathan and Abiram, God chooses the farmers. Dathan and Abiram complain that Moses has brought them to a land only good for farming. Where, they ask, is the good

15. Pardes, *Countertraditions in the Bible*, 2–3.

grazing land Moses had promised them? Here, God punishes the activist shepherds, calling on the fertile earth to swallow them up (Num 16:13–14).[16]

Finally, it's also possible Nadab and Abihu oppose the extravagance of the animal offerings. With prophetic vision, they see a possible future that undermines sustainable grazing. Eventually, local shepherds can't supply enough livestock for the *mishkan*. So, raising animals for ritual offerings becomes a lucrative business. A few wealthy ranchers with "factory farms" dominate the supply chain. The *mishkan* becomes a display of income inequality. Eventually, nothing is left of the old hands-on community project. It is replaced, perhaps, by something like King Solomon's Temple: a fancy house for God, funded by high taxes, and built by conscripted laborers.

When the prophets criticize the corruption of religion by wealth, some speak of exploited sheep. For example, Zechariah criticizes greedy shepherds who don't take care of their sheep or their underpaid workers (Zech 11). Ezekiel compares political leaders to cruel shepherds. They eat dairy and wear wool, but ignore the health of the flocks who produce them (Ezek 34:1–10). Obviously, neglected sheep is a prophetic metaphor for abused humans. But it is not just a metaphor; it also hints at a causal chain. Sheep are part of the local economic family. When you push them out of balance, you also harm their human kin.

No wonder the sheep sing, "Who is like you, YHWH?" In poetic form, they chant a shared history. *Remember, humans, when we were enslaved together—and then freed together? Together, we rise and fall and then rise again. Our fates are intertwined.*

16. Frankel, "Datan and Abiram."

Donkey

Spiritual Guide

UNDER BIBLICAL LAW, NO one has any rights. No one can claim anything from the community. That's just not the language biblical law uses. Instead, everyone has obligations towards others, because that's how community is built.[1] Human beings even have obligations towards donkeys. If you own a working donkey, you must let it rest one day a week (Deut 5:14; Exod 20:10). You must not force it to keep up with a gigantic ox (Deut 22:10). If you see a neighbor overworking their donkey, you are obliged to step in (Deut 22:4). When you see a donkey struggling under its load, you must help it directly, even if you hate its owner (Exod 23:5). If you help your enemy's donkey, rabbinic commentators add, you pave the way for peace, friendship, and community.[2]

Clearly, in the world of the Bible, donkeys are well-respected, highly valued working animals. They transport goods, carry riders, and, as an added benefit, provide spiritual guidance.[3] So, I want to talk about donkeys in the Bible from four perspectives: empirical, literary, magical, and meditative. Empirically, donkeys in Bible stories act like real donkeys. Literary patterns paint them as inner guides, perhaps even divine messengers. One magical

1. Holtz, "Reading Biblical Law," 2201; Messinger, "Rights and Responsibilities."

2. *Midrash Aggadah* on Exod 23:5.

3. As they do in modern times. See, for example, "In the Spirit of the Donkey."

donkey invites us to broaden our own perception of reality. Finally, the stories hint at a meditative spiritual practice for accessing our own inner guidance.

The Empirical Donkey

Recently, I visited the Turtle Valley Donkey Refuge in British Columbia, Canada. Our tour guide gave us a brief introductory talk. Donkeys are native to Africa, she said. They came to the Americas on Columbus's supply ships in 1495. Columbus expected to find active gold mines. He thought he would need donkeys to carry equipment, pull ore carts, and sire mules. Because donkey's hooves have excellent traction, they can work on many kinds of ground. Unfortunately, we know that Columbus found little gold.[4] And he did much killing of the Arawak people.[5]

Over time, donkeys became the North American "gold standard" of mining helpers. Donkeys served settlers through several gold rushes. Mules, offspring of a donkey and a mare, often worked in dangerous deep pit coal mines. "To a mine mule, nothing is impossible," wrote a reporter in 1884. Once a donkey or mule learns a task, the reporter said, it does it well. If an inexperienced driver makes a mistake, the animal will ignore the driver and do the job right. Most miners respected their working animals. So, typically, older donkeys and mules would retire to a farm.[6]

But, gradually, miners began to use steam engines to haul equipment and ore. Donkeys were no longer a good investment. So, some people simply abandoned their donkeys. Some donkeys, especially in arid areas, adapted. Due to their desert lineage, they are good at finding drinking water and, to keep cool, they coat themselves with dirt. But they need reliable rain shelters, as their hair doesn't repel water. And they need companions. So, those who formed herds survived. Some of those wild herds are still around.

4. Turtle Valley Donkey Refuge.
5. Casas and Griffin, *Destruction of the Indies*.
6. Sprowles, "Mine Mules."

Today in North America, outside of cities, donkeys are popular pets. One of my rural friends, while recovering from serious injury, adopted a donkey. As she slowly regained the use of her arms, she relied on him as a service animal. He took his job very seriously. So seriously, in fact, that he tried to do her reaching and lifting rehabilitation exercises *for her*! But donkeys live thirty-five to fifty years, and many outlive their owner-companions. Hence, the donkey refuge movement was born.

At the Turtle Valley Refuge, most donkeys were seniors. They moved slowly around their huge enclosure. But they all wandered up to the fence to meet us. They came in twos and threes, investigating us in small groups of close friends. The youngest and newest donkey, three years old, was in his own pen. "He came in full of himself," said the guide. "Till one of the older donkeys gave him a good punch in the nose!" He presented that nose to me, so I stroked it. Then, he turned his thick muscular neck towards me. To him, I wasn't a stranger, but a new friend. Equines communicate well through touch.[7] So, with my hand scratching his neck, we had a wordless conversation. Around us, the older donkeys began braying for their dinner, weaving a symphony of keys and rhythms. But my friend was not distracted; he stayed focused on our social task.

The Literary Donkey

Biblical donkeys, both male jacks and female jennies, often feature in what literary scholars call a "type scene." In everyday English, we might call it a "standard scene." Because it follows a culturally familiar outline, it cues readers to expect a certain plot point, and helps them connect emotionally with the characters. Still, storytellers play with minor variations, because surprises can delight readers, too. In modern films, we see type-scenes all the time: would-be lovers misinterpret cues; action heroes flee in improbable car chases; villains make long final confessions. Biblical writing

7. Hearne, *Adam's Task*, 107–8.

has its own stock of type-scenes. Future lovers meet at a well. Divine messengers predict a pregnancy. A dying hero instructs their heirs.[8] And—I'm adding a new one to the list—a distressed character travels with their donkey.

The typical donkey scene stars a human character who isn't sure where they are going or what they will do when they arrive. But, they saddle up their donkey, ride, and somehow find their way. The donkey type-scene draws on cultural views about donkeys in biblical times. Of course, biblical lawmakers and their publics respected donkeys for their physical skills: sure feet, strong back, adaptable diet. But they also valued donkeys' intellectual and moral qualities: quick learning, careful assessment of situations, and loyal support of a best friend.[9] These qualities that make donkeys good guides are subtly expressed in the type-scenes.

For example, when Abraham sets out to offer his son Isaac on the altar, he saddles his donkey and sets out. Abraham knows he is going to a place that God will show him, but he does not know where it is. So, he goes where his donkey takes him. But then, Abraham leaves the donkey with his servants. He walks on with Isaac and binds Isaac for slaughter on the altar. As Abraham raises the knife, he hears an angel call to him from the heavens, "Don't!" (Gen 22).

Abigail rides her donkey when she heads out to avert a massacre. Her churlish husband has insulted the outlaw David. So, David's gang is on its way to kill the man and all his farmworkers. Abigail has never met David, and she knows only that he is a very violent man. She does not know what she will say to appease him. But she saddles up her donkey and rides. As she dismounts, she finds the words that calm David down. In fact, her brief speech is a diplomatic masterpiece (1 Sam 25).

The unnamed woman from Shunem, a disciple of Elisha, the miracle-working man of God, relies on a donkey, too. When her son falls deathly ill, she rushes out to find Elisha. She saddles up her donkey and tells her servant not to interrupt her ride. When

8. Alter, *The Art of Biblical Narrative*, 55–57.
9. Viviers, "The 'Wonderful' Donkey."

the Shunamite reaches Elisha, she grasps his legs. She doesn't let him go until he agrees to travel with her and save her son's life (2 Kgs 4).

The pattern is clear. If you ride your donkey, who may be following God's directions,[10] you find your way. The inverse of the pattern holds true, too: if you lose your donkey, you go astray. When we readers first meet King Saul, he is on a mission to find his father's donkeys. Eventually he finds the prophet Samuel, who tells him, "Go home, your father's donkeys are found." Saul never finds the donkeys (1 Sam 9). Nor does he ever figure out how to be king. Swinging between courage and cowardice, love and hate, ferocity and compassion, his personal and political choices fail.

The judge Samson is a martial hero, but uncontrolled anger guides his strength. When his wife leaves him, he sets fire to fields owned by Philistines, using a strategy that also kills 300 foxes. In retaliation, the farmers kill Samson's wife; he beats them to death; avengers tie him up; and Samson attacks them with the bone of a dead donkey. Finally, Samson throws the bone away (Judg 15). At that point, Samson loses what little good sense he might have had. (Can you imagine the story's original audience nodding in agreement. "Yes, that's what happens when you lose your donkey!")

The Magical Donkey

The Bible's most famous donkey—Balaam's ride—stars in a special variation on the type-scene. The scene begins in a familiar way; then the unusual riffs show up. The Israelites, camped in the wilderness, develop a powerful army. The king of Moab fears them, so he tries to hire the seer Balaam to curse them. But God comes to Balaam in a dream and says, "Don't accept the job." So, Balaam declines to take it. Some time later, however, Balaam dreams again. In this dream God says, "Go. But do only what I tell you to do." So Balaam accepts the job. He saddles up his donkey and rides on out to work.

---

10. Way, "Animals in the Prophetic World," 53–54.

But, along the way, Balaam's donkey sees an angel holding a sword. So, she swerves off the path. Balaam tries to redirect her with a slap. But the angel moves, and narrows the path. The donkey adjusts, but traps Balaam's leg against a wall. He hits her again. Then, the angel moves again, blocking the path, and the donkey stops. Balaam hits her with a stick and curses her.

So, God opens her mouth, and she says, "What have I done to make you hit me three times?"

Balaam answers, "You mocked me! If I had a sword I would kill you."

But the donkey stays calm. "Aren't I *your* donkey, the one you've been riding for years? Is it my habit to do this?"

Balaam says, "No."

Then, his eyes open, he sees the angel, and bows low to the ground. The angel admonishes Balaam for beating his donkey, and paraphrases God's original message. "Go, but say only what I tell you to say" (Num 22).

Poor Balaam. Unlike the other riders, he does not trust his donkey. She offers direction, but he beats it down. Given the storyline, this is hardly a surprise. Balaam's inconsistent dreams show his inner struggles. God cannot reach him clearly on the dream wavelength. The usual donkey channel doesn't work either. Usually biblical donkeys guide subtly, simply by acting like donkeys. Their spiritual guidance folds into the fabric of everyday life. But Balaam's donkey has to step out of the ordinary to get Balaam's attention. So, she speaks out loud in Hebrew. And when she does, Balaam is not at all surprised.

Up to this point, Balaam's story has been realistic. Sure, characters believe in the power of dreams and curses, but that's just a human nature. When the donkey speaks, however, the story shifts into the genre of magical realism. Here, the story's overall setting is realistic, but magical things do happen, and characters simply accept them. Originally the term "magical realism" referred to visual art. A painter, for example, could make an ordinary object look extraordinary to us, so that we would never again see it in the same way. Literary stories of magical realism also aim at changing readers' perception. They turn our attention towards odd everyday experiences, socially marginalized voices, and different modes of consciousness.[11]

By now, you are thinking that the whole Bible uses the genre of magical realism. To be sure, within the Bible, it's not unusual for God or divinely inspired healers to do miraculous things. But when an ordinary animal or object does so, readers take notice. Classical rabbinic readers certainly did. One second-century text, *Pirkei Avot*, suggests that the Bible's magical realism shows us the edges of our world. This text lists ten biblical animals or objects, including "the mouth of the donkey," that do wondrous things. These "ten things were created on the eve of the [first] Shabbat at twilight."[12]

This pithy quotation holds a longer line of thinking. In the creation story told in Genesis 1, the world comes to be in an orderly manner over six days. Each day, God calls something into existence; it then exists; God declares it good; and the day ends. The day-to-day order is perfect, as each creature needs the environment created the previous day. The pattern results in a reliable natural world. But just as the sixth day is ending, just as work is mixing into rest, God sneaks in a few creatures that are outside the natural order. Still, they are part of God's world, as real as anything else!

If we look carefully, *Pirkei Avot* suggests, at twilight we can glimpse this magical reality. At twilight, day blends into night. Under odd purple skies, shadows dance in the dimming light. We see figures, and then, when we look again, they seem to have slipped away. Yesterday, for example, in the near-darkness, I saw hundreds of birds rising from the lake. Maybe these were only illusions. But maybe they were fragments of true perception. As the authoritative medieval scholar Rashi says, in his commentary on Balaam's donkey, spiritual beings do exist. But God did not give people the ability to see them. Such sights would be too confusing to rational

---

11. Zamora and Faris, *Magical Realism*, Kindle.
12. Kravitz and Olitzky, *M. Av* 5:6.

human minds. Instead, God gave this kind of vision to animals.[13] Of course, "animals" is quite a broad category, and Rashi should not make inferences about all non-humans based on one donkey. But Rashi is right that different species, who have different bodies, perceive the world differently. And that is why we occasionally need a donkey guide: to show us how to see more.

The Meditative Donkey

In a way, "riding the donkey" seems like a metaphor for developing spiritual perception. You saddle up, go on an inner journey, and return with deepened insight. To see the donkey stories this way, I read the text through a Hasidic lens. Hasidism was an eighteenth-century Jewish movement emphasizing what we might call "everyday Kabbalah," learning to see the divine in everyday life. Hasidic teachers used music, meditation, contemplation, prayer, and Torah study to help develop spiritual perception.[14] They learned to read the Bible as a kind of meditation manual. Instructions for spiritual practice, they taught, are metaphorically coded into characters, stories, and key phrases.

In the donkey type-scene, I see a basic template for a meditation technique that I like to call "riding the donkey." It has three steps: (1) saddle up; (2) ride; (3) dismount. What happens during step two, the ride, can be open-ended. You might, like the Shunamite woman, meet an inner teacher; or, like Balaam, perceive differently with your senses; or even, like Abigail, clarify emotions into a plan of action. But in every case, to "ride" safely and fruitfully, you need to create a ritual "container" for the ride.

First, you prepare, gradually moving out of ordinary consciousness. You may have a technique you've studied that always calms and focuses you, such as hatha yoga, deep breathing, chanting, or reading poetic psalms.[15]

---

13. *Mikraot Gedolot,* Rashi on Num 22:23.
14. Duhan-Kaplan, "Vibration of the Other," 119.
15. Duhan-Kaplan, *The Infinity Inside,* 25–30.

Second, when you feel your thought and feeling have changed, you can let go of the practice, and "ride," so to speak, on the saddle you have prepared. As you ride, stay with the type of experience that has come forward. You might sit with feelings, listen to sounds, recall a dream from the night before, look more impartially than usual on memories that surface, allow concepts of infinity to stretch your thought. At some point, you may feel you have "arrived" at a destination. You may have received an insight, a perceptual shift, a feeling of well-being, a life-question for further thought, a memory newly resurfaced.

Third, when you arrive, you "dismount," and take some time to articulate where you landed. You might journal, draw, talk to God, or make notes to bring to your next conversation with a spiritual friend or spiritual director. When you dismount in this way, you may notice deeper dimensions of the ride. Try to make time for all three steps; it is a powerful process. It is also helpful to let go of preconceptions or plans about where your meditation will lead you. Remember, the donkey ride works best when you believe in your journey, even if you don't quite know where you are doing, or what you will do when you get there.

No wonder later biblical writers—both Jewish and Christian—associate donkeys with hope, divine guidance, and messianic time. Both the prophet Zechariah (Zech 9:9) and, after him, the gospel writer Matthew (Matt 21:1–11), see the Messiah entering Jerusalem on a donkey. Scholars and preachers wonder if the donkey is one or two, white or rainbow-colored, an image of spiritual royalty or working-class power.[16] But all agree: humanity can stand to take direction from the donkey's unique blend of stability, loyalty, and intuition.

---

16. See, for example *b. Sanh.* 98a; Almalech, "Biblical Donkey"; Bedard, "Did Jesus Ride Two Donkeys?"; Patta, "Palm Sunday: A Celebration of Political Hegemony."

Corvid

Friend and Scout

A FAMOUS HAIDA LEGEND tells us how raven steals the light.[1] Raven lives among humans as a baby, opens a puzzle box filled with light, and then takes off to soar on his own. This mythical raven is, in fact, a lot like actual ravens and crows. They solve problems and fly high. But, more significantly, they both are and are not part of human society. Crows have colonized our city and yes, this has involved them bullying out some other species. They have divided our city into family territories. There, in summer, pairs of parents and their still-single young adult children raise babies. In winter, they forage there by day, and join the larger crow community at night. Species norms tell them when it is okay to enter another's territory. Many humans don't know how crows live. But crows definitely know about human life. Crows keep a keen eye on their territories, and know a great deal about the individual humans who live there. If something is out of order, they notice. Their social lives are, in many ways, similar to ours. Thus, I suggest, we can learn a lot from them about mutual support.

Corvid: Bird of the Evening

In Vancouver, where I live, crows own the evening sky. Every evening, as pink light fades to purple, 6,000 of these crows head home.

1. Reid and Bringhurst, *The Raven Steals the Light*, 19–24.

They leave their day jobs of foraging in family territories. Together, they return to a communal roost in the trees by Still Creek, in the eastern suburb of Burnaby.[2] And every evening, a million human heads look up and watch the winged parade. Crows are simply part of our urban landscape. Last May, crows nested outside my office window. The year before, outside our home's back door. The crows befriended us after we protected their nest from predators. Then, they showed up every day for a peanut snack. Eventually, they brought their young teen to meet us. This is not an unusual crow-human collaboration. But crows can also be sensitive. Each June, the local community college compiles a list of sites where crows attack.[3] We try to avoid these places. Obviously, adults there are protecting hidden vulnerable fledglings.

My husband Charles and I love to watch crows on their evening flight home.[4] One evening, we drove out to Burnaby to watch the 6,000 crows gather at their roost. The gathering was part theatre, part horror movie, and thoroughly real life. Crow central is busy and intense. To make sense of what we're seeing, we human visitors rely on past associations and images. So, I delighted as group after group of dancers performed improvisational aerial ballet. Charles cringed as rows of alien creatures with swords for mouths stood at attention on tree branches. And we both covered our ears, because crows tend to yell when they're in a crowd.

We have ravens in our city, too, though urban ravens are unusual. Usually, crows prefer human environments. Ravens, normally rural animals, only tolerate them. Crows often show up to help other crows defend their family territories. But ravens are strict about keeping other ravens out. Both gather in big groups at night, but crow groups are ten times as large as raven groups.[5] It's easy to tell crows and ravens apart once you see them together. And once you recognize the raven's throaty trill, you will never confuse the two species again. Usually, we hear them scolding each other.

2. McLachlan, "Where Do Those Crows Go?"
3. O'Leary, "CrowTrax."
4. Macdonald, "In the Company of Crows."
5. Swift, "In the Company of Corvids."

Crows don't like that ravens eat their nestlings.[6] Ravens don't like that crows try to dominate compost bins. They only work together to banish bald eagles from their territories (see the eagle chapter).

Despite these differences, Biblical Hebrew has only one word for both birds. Members of the corvid family of birds, which includes both crows and ravens, are all called *orev*. This Hebrew word is spelled with the letters *ayin, resh, bet*. Depending on vowel markings that affect pronunciation, the word can also mean "evening," "mixture," and "pleasant." But early Hebrew texts do not have vowel markings. Fluent readers can tell from the context which pronunciation is correct. But we can still see multiple meanings at play. In fact, the word *orev* beautifully describes a singular moment of the day. As the sky is lit with *mixed* colors, gradually *evening* into midnight blue, *corvids* fly overhead, *pleasing* their amazed human fans.

Biblical writers, I'm sure, were familiar with this time of day. In telling the story of creation, they have to strike a delicate balance. The story takes place in a mostly empty world. But the audience draws its vocabulary from a fully created world. At the end of creation's first day, only light and dark exist. Sun, moon, and stars, our usual markers of time, do not. How, then, can the writers describe the passage of time with the tools they have? And in a way that foreshadows a future lived human rhythm? They choose to draw on the wordplay of *ayin, resh, bet*. "It was evening, it was morning," they say, *vayehi erev, vayehi boker* (Gen 1:5). Light *mixed* into dark. The effect was *pleasant*. We call it *evening*. And, in the future, this will be flight time for the *corvid*. The writers try a similar wordplay for the morning. The letters of *boker—bet, kuf, resh*—also spell *bakar*, cattle. In the future, morning will be early chore time for farmers and ranchers.

6. Duhan-Kaplan, "Crows Are Nesting in Our Backyard!"

Corvids and Humans

If you catch crows in a small group, in a quiet spot, at a peaceful time of day, you may overhear a conversation—like I did at Scott's Bay, Nova Scotia. The words were crow vocalizations: caws, cackles, and odd rolling sounds. But they were arranged unmistakably into sentences, shared in the give and take of conversation. Biologists have documented and begun to analyze this language.[7] No doubt some humans have mastered it. I haven't—yet. Sometimes, in the city, I speak the sounds of crow language. Surely, the content of what I say is nonsense. "Feed the pumpkin in your grab bag," or something like that. But crows take notice. One of our neighborhood crows is highly sensitive, and thus easily agitated. Recently, I came upon it screaming, pumping its chest and wings. But when I clicked and clacked a string of sounds, it calmed down immediately.

Biologists have also reported on corvids' sophisticated problem-solving skills, and praised corvid intelligence.[8] Many of us have seen this in action! I have learned, for example, that if you're in trouble in the wilderness, ravens may rescue you. They rescued me from a foolish adventure in Colorado: a solo hike across windy tundra at 12,000 feet, on my first day out, with my lungs still operating at low sea-level efficiency. After only an hour, my thinking wasn't linear, my hands and feet were tingling, my swollen limbs were triggering my chronic nerve pain. When I tried to write in my journal, illegible scrawling came out. I must have looked pretty bad. And suddenly, I heard, "Croa-oa-oa!" A raven was calling. A passing flock of three had slowed to a circle and was trying to get my attention. I tried to focus through the mental fog and I made a plan: put one foot in front of the other, stumble back to the trail, walk to the road, drive to the ranger station, ask for oxygen. The ravens escorted me until I reached the trail. No wonder both Noah and Elijah rely on corvids!

7. Marzluff, *In the Company of Crows and Ravens*, 196–217.
8. Savage, *Bird Brains*.

Noah's Scout and Elijah's Helper

In the biblical story of Noah's Ark, most of the animals merely have walk-on parts, so to speak. Noah and family gather them into the safety of a giant boat just before a great flood begins. Only two animals have significant roles: *Orev* and *Yonah*, the dove. After forty days of continuous rain and then months of floating, Noah decides to check the global water level. He sends *Orev* on a reconnaissance mission. *Orev* flies out and back until the waters recede. Next, Noah sends the dove. She cannot find a perch, so she comes home and perches on Noah's arm. Seven days later, Noah sends her out again, and she returns with a torn olive leaf. Seven days later, Noah sends her out again, and she does not return (Gen 8:6–12).

When we imagine this scene, we draw on our associations and images of these birds. As a child, I only knew *Orev* as a shouting, mobbing bird. So, when I read about *Orev*'s role on the ark, I imagined him as crazy and stubborn. He misunderstands his mission; he flies around in circles; He's no help to Noah whatsoever. But then the sweet dove gets it right. No wonder she's the ancestor of the homing pigeon.

But now, as an adult, I understand *Orev*'s skill set. Each morning, he heads out on his own and each evening he returns to his large flock to debrief the day. As research biologists know, he speaks a complex language woven of words, syntax, and gestures. He can learn human words, and use them correctly in new situations. His range includes every earthly landscape, from high alpine tundra to low seaside grove. And he's a keen observer of human life.[9] Obviously, Noah sends *Orev* on a mission that *Orev* completes perfectly: to fly out and return each day with a report. That's how Noah knows when there is enough dry ground to send out a dove. Her mission is to use her good sense of direction and keen eye to finding nesting materials on the ground.

Early rabbinic commentators, writing 1,500 years ago, knew about the range of human responses to *Orev*. Their creative commentaries acknowledge both negative and positive views of *Orev*.

9. Haupt, *Crow Planet*, 8.

One midrash in *Genesis Rabbah* describes a Noah who dislikes corvids. It imagines the following conversation.

Orev asks Noah, "Why send me on this dangerous solo mission?"

Noah answers, "You're not kosher, so I can't eat you or offer you as a sacrifice. What good are you to the world? Who cares if you don't return?"

But God intervenes to educate Noah and says, "One day, *Orev* will feed a righteous human being."[10]

The author of this midrash connects two corvid stories. The first, obviously, takes place on Noah's Ark. The second is set many years later, in the time of the Israelite kings. Because of greedy King Ahab, no rain is falling. Food is scarce and people are starving. The prophet Elijah publicly criticizes the king. So, for Elijah's safety, God instructs him to go into hiding. No one has the resources to feed a dissident in hiding—except the *Orev* family by the river (1 Kgs 17:6).

Being corvids, these activists do not worry about the king's power. They strictly control their own territory, and wisely cache their extra food. So, when God tells them to feed Elijah, they do it. They are heroes modeling political activism when most humans are not up to the task. This midrash from the *Genesis Rabbah* compilation fits right into that collection's main theme. *Genesis Rabbah* presents one key message in multiple variations: God created the universe as a well-ordered web of cause and effect. That web supports the Jewish people. God has placed in the world everything they need to survive threatening times.[11] So, *orev* is here to teach us about quiet grassroots activism—how to organize in groups, regardless of differences, and support one another.

Another midrash presents Noah as more neutral towards corvids. He and *Orev* are discussing the reconnaissance mission. *Orev* believes it is dangerous and does not want to go. He tries to talk Noah out of it.

---

10. *Bereisheet Rabbah* 33:5 on Gen 8:7.

11. Neusner, *Rabbinic Literature,* 355–81.

"Noah," *Orev* says, "you brought only two of my species onto this boat. If I go out and something happens to me, my mate will be alone and my species will cease to exist. Or have you already thought of that? Are you sending me away so that you can marry my mate?"

But Noah insists that no mating can take place in the crowded ark. "I haven't even had sex with my wife; so I certainly wouldn't do that with yours!" Dismissing the objection, Noah insists that *Orev* fly out.[12]

When I first read this midrash, I was shocked that our sages thought Noah was so clueless about *Orev's* worries. Of course, a lonely social bird might adopt a human mate. Years ago, my quaker parrot tried to push my husband out of the picture and adopt me! *Orev* probably assumes Noah might do the same. Noah, the animal expert, should understand this.

But then I remembered that the midrash isn't really about Noah. It's about importing lessons from Noah's story into other times and places. The midrash about *Orev* helping Elijah teaches about activism in times of oppression. Similarly, the midrash about mating looks towards a time of mass species extinction. In Noah's story, wicked human behavior caused a catastrophic climate event. Survivors wait, wondering when their habitat might recover. In the meantime, no one reproduces; all face possible extinction. They wonder if new species who can adapt might emerge. Finally, someone sets aside their fears and flies out to glimpse the future: *Orev*.

We should all learn from *Orev's* character. Physically, *Orev* is nothing like a human being. But his intelligence and personal concerns are similar. And he is a visionary. He believes in treating other species like family. And, despite his worries, he risks his personal well-being for the good of all. As Genesis 1:5 hints, this kind of steadiness can keep the cycles of nature going. "It was *erev;* it was morning; one day."

12. *b. Sanh.* 108b.

Snake

A Different Way of Life

UNLIKE CROWS, SNAKES DON'T generally share their lives with humans. But the Bible suggests that they once did. So, let's visit the Garden of Eden. We'll peek in on the first humans and the first snake. But, to see them clearly, we'll have to bracket our familiar interpretations. You may have learned the view of medieval Christian writer Augustine. The snake tempted the humans to disobey God and fall into sin.[1] Or maybe you learned the view of medieval Jewish writer Maimonides. The snake led the humans to activate their intellects and live more deeply into the divine image.[2] Right now, it does not matter which you learned. Set them both aside, and look at the Garden through a different lens. Imagine that the world is very new. Species don't yet know themselves. Their bodies and their way of life are mysterious to them. And the younger the species, the less they know. So they experiment. And some of the early experiments are a bit odd. But the first trials and errors don't doom the creatures, or mark them with a permanent nature. Instead they learn about themselves and others. So, try reading the Garden of Eden story as a quirky comedy about a world finding its way. But first I'll explain how I came to see it in that mode.

---

1. Bonaiuti and La Piana, "St. Augustine's Idea of Original Sin."
2. Maimonides, *Guide for the Perplexed*, 1:1.

Evolution

Ten years ago, my husband and I visited the *Blue Beach Fossil Museum and Research Station* at the Bay of Fundy, Nova Scotia. At that time, it was a deeply hidden national treasure. You couldn't find it by following road signs. You had to use curiosity, intuition, and hope. So, we drove down an unmarked dirt road. Then, we walked along an unmarked dirt path. Finally, we reached a clearing. An unpaved parking lot in front of a big old barn.

An elderly dog waddled out to meet us. Her body was misshapen and scarred from illness and injury. But every detail of her body language said, "Welcome!"

An older gentleman was dancing to silent music. Suddenly he pulled off his headphones.

"Have you heard the latest Frank Zappa Concert?" he asked.

Given that Zappa had been dead for thirteen years, I said, "No."

"Phew!" he said. "Because the lyrics about people in the backseat of a car might be a little over the top for you!"

A woman in a motorized wheelchair was packing boxes into a van. She reminded the gentleman that we probably wanted to see the museum. So, the dog took her cue. She led us to a big old barn, filled with rocks, boxes of rocks, piles of rocks, and posters about rocks.

A skinny younger man appeared, probably from a hidden back room. His clothes were filthy and he smelled like cigarettes. He was our tour guide. For the next forty-five minutes, he talked without a pause. The dog lay down at the edge of the barn, overseeing the tour. Clearly, she was the staff member in charge.

In those forty-five minutes, we learned seven amazing facts.

1. Beach fossils are discovered when soft slabs of shale are split apart.

2. Each side of the imprint carries different information.

3. Anyone can find a beach fossil if they know how to look.

4. Schoolchildren visiting the museum have made important finds.

5. The local fossil record documents a unique time in the evolution of amphibious animals, when members of a single species began to change, with some living in the water and some living on land.

6. Often, university scientists get a grant to visit a research station for a few days. Then, they write an article and get credit for the work done by the resident researchers.

7. Our tour guide, however, did co-author an article about the amphibians, and it should be coming out soon.

A few weeks later, we were delightfully surprised to read an article about him in our local newspaper. Chris Mansky had indeed co-authored a scientific paper presenting new evidence about amphibian evolution. And, now, the museum is evolving, too. There's a fancy web page, a site renovation plan, and a non-profit society with a fundraising plan. Scientists from around the world visit. Mr. Mansky and his wife Sonja Woods have been celebrated in national news. A paleontologist honoured him by naming a newly discovered fish species "Avonichthys Manskyi."[3] Still, I keep thinking of Manksy's simplest teaching. *Anyone can find a beach fossil if they know where to look.* Even children!

A Changing Creation

People in biblical times lived near shorelines. Surely, they, too, could find fossils. Some, I imagine, they could easily identify. Local fish, trapped long ago at low tide, who never made it back out to sea. But surely biblical naturalists also found fossils of unfamiliar species. What did they make of those? And when they found shellfish fossils way out in the desert—like the ammonites at the Ramon Crater—what did they conclude? Surely they understood that landscapes change. And that species adapt to their environments.

But I'm not just imagining this. I'm also following the clues that biblical writers left. In the Genesis story, specifically, they hint at species change. Of course they don't present anything like a

3. Thomson, "Ancient Fish Species Discovered."

modern theory of evolution. There's no phylogenetic map showing how species descend from one another. No clear theory of adaptation, like Darwin's natural selection or Lamarck's inheritability. But the potential for change is built into every plant and animal species. And there may even have been a primordial time when species were very much in flux. You can find these hints in both creation stories.

Genesis begins with two creation narratives. Both stories describe our world and its creatures. But they have different feeling-tones. So, they represent two ideas of how the world came to be. The first story (Gen 1:1—2:3) moves from chaos to stability. God creates the world step by interlocking step. Each step is good; the last step is very good; the final pause is holy. God speaks and things happen, as if an unseen staff of thousands implements each command. Humans are created at once male and female, and God welcomes them with a blessing of abundance. The second story (Gen 2:4—3:24) begins with emptiness. God then fills it in a disorderly way, making experiments and adjustments. The narrator notes that gold, the precious metal, is good, but nothing else seems to stand out. Sometimes, God works like an artist or a farmer, shaping clay into creatures with unseen hands. Eventually, God creates a man and welcomes him with a job description and a warning; later, God creates a woman. When the two humans ignore the warning, God introduces them to a harsh life of scarcity and struggle.

You can put the stories side by side in many different ways. For example, you can harmonize them, saying that the first story gives the broad outlines, and the second fills in the details. Or you can contrast them, saying the first describes God's ideal world, while the second describes our real human world. You can imagine attitudes of two different first women, Lilith, proudly equal, and Eve, sadly subservient. Or find traces of two different authors' styles. Learning from all these approaches, I'll both compare and contrast. So, I'll note a common theme in both stories: flexibility of species. But each story explores it in a unique literary way. The first creation story presents an orderly, poetic narrative, with hints of change peeking through the formal structure. In contrast, the second story is ironic and humorous. Confusion and instability among species are its main points. And it all centers around the snake, of course. But we'll get there, soon.

Seeds of Future Generations

To see the theme in the first creation story, you have to pay careful attention to the poetry. Specifically, to the contrast between stability and change in the writing. Notice what quickly becomes predictable, and then what new ideas show up. Start with the lines that form the daily framework of the story.

> God said, let there be . . .
> and there was . . .
> God saw that it was good . . .
> It was evening, it was morning, day [number].

There's an orderly rhythm to this creation. An instruction is issued, carried out, evaluated. Completion is logged and time stamped. Everything happens at God's word, in God's time, and in a good way. And, if you follow early rabbinic interpretation, according to God's plan.[4] Because each new creature makes possible what comes after it. God creates seas before creating fish. Patches of land among the waters before plants. Sky before sun, moon, and stars. Fruits and vegetables before animals. And then, and only then, human beings.

But tucked between the orderly lines of this framework, there's a surprising word that shows up ten times. It's *zera*, seed. It pops up, so to speak, in several grammatical variants. And it sows a bit of chaos in the order. A seed is bundle of raw materials with a built-in blueprint. In the right conditions, it will grow into something like its parent plant. But it won't be exactly like its parent. It may scatter in the wind. Sprout in strange soil. Grow differently in its new surroundings. And that, says Genesis 1, is what God intended. A world in which species can change in unpredictable ways.

4. *Bereisheet Rabbah* 1:1 on Gen 1:1.

The Human Experiment

In the second creation story, unpredictability is the whole point. There's no rhythm and no plan. God seems to stumble from experiment to experiment, figuring things out as they happen. In this story, God has no concept of what a species is, how it sustains itself, or how it reproduces. To begin, God creates grain-producing grasses. But of course, they can't grow, because God hasn't made any rains or farmers. So, God fixes both problems. A spring comes up from the land to water the ground. And then, God forms an *adam*, a human, with dust from the *adamah,* the soil's organic humus. Finally, God blows into it a breath of life. The human–humus connection is a pun that works in both English and Hebrew. Initially, *Adam* isn't a proper name; it's just what the first human is, an earthling. But when a second human is born, *Adam* becomes the first human's name. The second human . . . well, we'll get to her name, soon.

God plants a garden in *Eden* (delight), at the headwaters of four rivers, near lands rich in good gold and precious gems. In this garden, every tree is delightful to look at and good to eat. God places the human in the garden to work and protect it. But—in contrast with the first creation story in which God explains to humans their life purpose—God only gives the human one instruction. "Eat from any tree in the garden." But perhaps that is not enough instruction, because God quickly adds a qualifier. "But don't eat from the tree of knowing good and bad, for on the day you eat from it, you'll surely die" (Gen 2:16–17).

Next, God says, perhaps as a personal reflection on the project so far, "It's not good for the human to be alone. I'll make it a helper, a parallel being" (Gen 2:18). So, using the humus, God forms animals and birds. But, it seems, God is not sure whether any of them will be the right match. So God brings these creatures to the human, to see what the human will call out to them. The human calls out, and the calls become the animals' names. But the human does not call out "Hello, mate!" to any of them. Because, it turns out, none of these species is the right mate.

So, God tries another experiment. Using material from the sleeping human's body, God creates another human. When the first human wakes, it says, "This time! It's the *etzem me'atazmay!*" Bone of my bone! Strength of my strength! Substance of my substance! This one will be called woman, because this one was taken out of a man" (Gen 2:23). Once again, it seems, God was not sure how well the experiment would work. But this time, the human calls out the right words. "We have the same essence! We are two genders of a single species!" Finally, things are simple and clear. Or to put it metaphorically, as the Bible does, the two humans may be naked, but they're not confused.

Snake: The Self-Appointed Standard

Enter the snake. It is the most *arum* of all the land animals (Gen 3:1). The Hebrew word *arum* means both "prudent" and "naked." And here it makes sense to convey both meanings, because snakes are both prudent and naked. Today, there are at least 3,000 species of snakes in the world. No two are exactly alike, but snake life does have some themes.

Arum can describe the snake's prudent life-strategy. Snakes are efficient animals. Many are ambush predators, who rest, camouflaged, waiting for their prey to wander by.[5] Snakes often wait under leaves or dirt, where they have little use for vision. So, their eyesight is not keen. But, they do hear, in a way. They feel vibrations as their prey approaches. And, because they are ectothermic animals who warm themselves in the sun, their heat sensors are strong.[6] So they track their prey by its heat signature. Then, they eat their weekly or monthly meal, converting 80 percent of it to body mass. As one snake enthusiast said of her pet ball python, "She can't be a glutton; mercy is built into her eating process. She is beautifully efficient."[7]

5. Lillywhite, *How Snakes Work*, 22.
6. Steen, *Secrets of Snakes*, 46.
7. Wallace, "Interview."

Arum also hints at the way snakes grow—by getting naked. As a snake gets bigger, the top layer of its skin stretches. When the skin reaches its limit, the snake gets ready to shed it. As the outer skin loosens, fluid collects underneath it, and the snake's eyes turn blue, its body cloudy. The snake will rub its face against a rough object to loosen the skin. And then, it will gradually wriggle out.[8] Snakes shed four to twelve times a year; the process takes a few days. "I'm jealous," says my snake-loving friend. "Shedding seems refreshing."[9]

The biblical snake visits the humans, and strikes up a conversation. He seems quite curious about them. Such strange creatures, he must wonder. What life instructions did the Creator give them? Do they, like me, eat small animals and avoid fruit? So the snake asks the woman, "Did God also say [to you], don't eat from any trees in the garden?" No, answers the woman, "we do feed on the garden trees." But then, trying to find some kinship with the snake, she explains that God did also tell the humans to avoid some trees. "But about the fruit of the tree in the middle, God said not to eat from it and not to touch it, to avoid the risk of dying" (Gen 3:2–3).

Not to touch it! Of course this seems wrong to the snake. He can't even grow unless he touches the tree. To start his shed, he rubs against the branch. And, in fact, the woman *is* mistaken. God gave the first human life instructions: don't eat from the tree. But she, the woman, was not yet born. So, how did she find out? Did God repeat the instructions to the woman? Did the man tell her? The narrator doesn't answer those questions. We only learn that the woman gets them wrong.

So, the snake offers a little mentoring—at least, from a snake's point of view. He realizes the woman has not heard well. Maybe she is preparing to shed her skin. So, she might have a little fluid in her ears. Whatever the reason, one thing is clear: she does not know the good way to live. So, the snake coaches her on what he thinks God intended. "You won't 'surely die,'" he says. "God knows that on the day you eat from it, your eyes will be opened, and you'll

8. Maclaine, *Snakes*, 4.
9. Wallace, "Interview."

be, like God, knowers of [what's] good and bad" (Gen 3:1, 4–5). Or, in other words: let the tree help you. Start your shed, free up your eyes, and let your body grow. Then you'll begin to understand how your species should live.

The woman checks out the fruit, using her most powerful human sense: sight. "She *sees* that the fruit is good for eating and desirable to the *eyes*." She wants to know about life, and she now sees that "the tree is delightful for knowing" (Gen 3:6). So she eats, and gives some to her man, who is with her. He also eats. And, suddenly, something changes. Their eyes open, and they see that they, like the snake, are now *eirumim,* naked and prudent. It's as if they have shed their skin and removed the cloudy membrane from their eyes. They are refreshed, physically and mentally. Now they know the good way to live—they think.

The humans now begin to act like snakes. They no longer rely on sight, but on their snake senses, reacting to vibration and temperature. They hear the sound of God walking in the garden at the breezy time of day. Like shy snakes, they hide themselves in a garden tree. God, it seems, does not expect this response. So, God calls out, "Where are you?" The man says, "I heard your voice in the garden and I was afraid because I'm *eirom.* So I hid myself." God wonders how this change of consciousness has come about. So, God asks, "Who told you you're *eirom*? Did you eat from the tree I told you not to eat from?" Well, yes, I did, the man says. And here's how it happened. "The woman you placed with me, she gave to me from the tree and I ate." Still a bit puzzled, God turns to the woman and asks, "What is this you did?" She says, "The snake raised me up and I ate."

Ah! God now understands. The snake has shared its life wisdom. But this wisdom is not right for humans. For the same reason, in fact, that the snake was not the right mate for a human. They are, it turns out, different species. As God sets out to remind them all. You, snake, will slither on your belly. And those little bony spurs on the back of your spine? (Yes, snakes are classified as four-limbed tetrapods, and some species do have vestigial legs.)[10]

10. Lillywhite, *How Snakes Work,* 5.

The bones won't be growing into legs, like the humans have, anytime soon. So, just stop hanging out with the humans. From now on, only their heels will come into contact with your head.

You, woman, you will not give birth as a snake does. You won't have dozens of babies at once. Every single one will be hard work. And there will be no parthenogenesis for you. (Yes, several snake species can do this.) You'll always need your human mate. And if you want more life wisdom from an older creature? Get it from him, because *hu yimshol bakh* (Gen 3:16). Usually, the phrase is translated "he will rule (*yimshol*) over you." But the root of *yimshol*, i.e., *mashal*, also means wise proverb.[11] Thus, says God, your man, not the snake, should teach you the good way to live.

And you, human man, don't copy the snake either. You won't be an ambush predator. No, you won't get to lie in wait for your meal to come to you. Instead, you'll have to pull grain out of the parched ground, and work up a sweat turning it into bread.

In response, the human man does not challenge or argue. But he does enact a very small resistance. Because he has the power to call out and name, he names his wife. He calls her *Khava* (Eve), an old Aramaic word for "snake."[12] Next, God creates robes made of skin, and dresses the humans. They won't shed again. Their time of experimentation is over. But its memory lives on in Eve's name.

11. Mimi Feigelson, "Wisdom."
12. *Bereisheet Rabbah* 20:11 on Gen 3:20.

Eagle

Metaphor and Spiritual Perception

IN THE TEN COMMANDMENTS, God explicitly forbids making images of the divine (Exod 20:4). But, traditionally, interpreters say God forbids only physical images.[1] Literary metaphors for God are welcome. A metaphor—according to one definition—is a figure of speech that talks about one thing in terms of another. When we hear the metaphor, we look at both terms just a bit differently.[2] So, each metaphor teaches about God, and also about God's reflection in created things. Still, core teachers, including Maimonides, remind us not to take the metaphors literally.[3]

One of my favorite biblical metaphors for God is the eagle. After the exodus, God says, "I carried you on eagles' wings" (Exod 19:4). Before Moses dies, he reminds the Israelites that God cares for them as eagle "hovers" *(yerakhef)* over its nestlings (Deut 32:11). Similarly, in the first creation story, the spirit of God "hovers" *(merakhefet)* over the primordial waters (Gen 1:2). These metaphors build on our knowledge of the natural environment. But they also push us to learn more. They reframe what we know, so we see familiar things differently. They nudge our consciousness into a new kind of perception. Some teachers even say that eagle metaphors are about the transformation of consciousness!

1. Halbertal and Margalit, *Idolatry,* 37–66.
2. Black, *Models and Metaphors,* 39–44; "More about Metaphor," 19–43.
3. Maimonides, *Guide for the Perplexed,* "Introduction."

Eagle Myths and Realities

Years ago, I knew little about bald eagles. When I was a child, I rarely saw them. Poisoned by pesticides, they were an endangered species. But their well-being is now protected under U.S. and Canadian law, and by the practices of some Indigenous nations. Bald eagles, much easier to find now, shine in photo essays, like Stan Tekiela's *Majestic Eagles*.[4] They star in personal accounts of friendship written by wildlife rehabilitators like Jeff Guidry and Brenda Cox.[5] Some, due to injuries, live in wildlife sanctuaries. When our children were young, we went regularly to the Carolina Raptor Centre. There, forested paths led us past little huts outfitted with different bird habitats to a final, dramatic exhibit. This was, of course, a giant enclosure for permanently injured bald eagles. Despite their territorial impulses, the group had somehow figured out how to live together. Our family would sit, in wonder, listening to the eagles' high-pitched chittering sounds. How could such large, powerful birds sing like little glass bells?

But I see bald eagles regularly now. Every fall, they migrate to our coastal region, hoping to feast on the spawning salmon. Now, I don't wonder at the eagle's voice; I just recognize it. Of course, I still love to watch eagles soar as high as 10,000 feet, and I'm excited for every opportunity. I'm fascinated by the broad platform nests parents build high in the trees, the months they spend raising their young, and the young eagles' four-year adolescent walkabout. But, I'm angry when bald eagles taunt my local crow friends or threaten small dogs. And I'm bemused when I drive by the local landfill. Each winter, thousands of bald eagles gather to rest at our landfills. With food so plentiful, fierce family territorial behaviors fall away. The regular landfill eagles can't even understand why newcomers hang onto old competitive habits.[6]

4. Tekiela, *Majestic Eagles*.

5. Guidry, *An Eagle Named Freedom*; Cox, *Conversations with an Eagle*.

6. Elliot, et al. "Foraging Ecology of Bald Eagles"; Pynn, "Ladner Landfill Becomes Bald Eagle Haven"; House, "BC Elder Talks about Eagles."

So, eagles are part of my habitat, as they were part of the biblical landscape. Thus, I know just enough to be trusted with these biblical metaphors. As I read them, God means, "I made you soar above all danger." Moses means, "God taught us carefully, then released us to wander and learn." And Genesis means, "God's spirit tended the world as it incubated." But one well-cited commentator knows very little about raptors. So, he takes the metaphor literally, and tries to infer biological facts from it. Most birds, says this Rabbi Eliezer, carry their babies in their feet. That's how they protect the babies from high-flying raptors. But the eagle flies so high, it has no aerial predators. It alone among birds can carry babies on its shoulders. And thus it also protects them from human hunters below.[7] Clearly, Rabbi Eliezer is moved by the metaphor's hint at God's power and love. But, biologically, most of what he says is wrong, even upside down. Some raptors carry prey in their talons, but it's hardly a loving act. And no birds, as far as we know, carry babies in their feet. Some birds do actually carry babies on their backs—but they are not the high flyers. Rather, they are low floating water birds.[8]

Eagle, Vulture, or Condor?

Technically speaking, the *nesher,* the biblical eagle, isn't exactly an eagle. More likely, the Hebrew word *nesher* means "vulture."[9] But English translators, beginning with Wycliffe in the fourteenth century and continuing with King James in the seventeenth century,[10] preferred to construe it as an "eagle." Culturally, they made a good choice. Shakespeare's sixteenth-century English gives us a hint of why.[11] Eagles, his plays suggest, are fierce, keen-eyed,

7. *Mechilta de Rabbi Shimon b. Jochai* 19 on Exod 19:4; *Mikraot Gedolot,* Rashi on Deut 32:1.

8. Ehrlich, Dobkin, and Wheye, "Transporting Young."

9. Slifkin, *Perek Shira,* 220–22.

10. Bible Gateway, search on Exod 19:4.

11. Proudfoot, Thompson, and Kastan, eds. *Shakespeare: Complete Works.* See, for example, on the eagle, *Titus Andronicus,* 4.4.85–88; *Richard II,* 3.3.74–76;

soaring birds. Vultures are unkind, devouring carrion from the inside out. So, in English, "eagle" absolutely conveys divine majesty, and "vulture" absolutely does not.

In Biblical Hebrew, *nesher*, likely the griffon vulture, is the king of birds. Griffon vultures outdo eagles in their size, wingspan, and soaring height. Modern researchers have recorded the griffon vulture flying at 37,000 feet, as high as a commercial airplane. Ecological philosopher David Abram writes beautifully about the mystique of high-flying birds in the Himalayan hills. As they soar, they see over rock formations and mountain peaks. In such a landscape, Abram says, "those who dwell and soar in the sky are the primary powers." When one lammergeier condor approached, Abram was transfixed by its huge size, hovering presence, and clear gaze. Abram felt himself brought to a deeper life by the aura of this alien intelligence.[12]

No wonder biblical poets were moved to speak of God as a vulture! Intelligent, powerful, heavenly, and all-seeing, the vulture nudges you into a higher consciousness. But in some modern spiritual poetry, that's exactly what the eagle does. For example, American Poet Laureate Joy Harjo of the Muscogee nation writes about attuning to the gliding of an eagle. If we allow ourselves to feel into its gentle circles, she says, we will become aware of all kinds of circles: our ecosystem, the pattern of our breath, the cycles of life and death. The eagle opens us to a higher awareness.[13]

Kabbalah: Eagle Wings

Some teachers of Kabbalah also see the eagle metaphor as a teaching about awareness.[14] Their Hasidic teaching riffs on Moses'

Cymbeline, 5.4.119–24. On the vulture, see *King Lear*, 2.4.124–27; *Macbeth*, 4.3.85–87; *Titus Andronicus*, 5.2.33–35.

12. Abram, *Spell of the Sensuous,* 21–22.

13. Harjo, "Eagle Poem."

14. Paltiel, "Kinesher Yair Kino." Here, I offer my gloss on Rabbi Paltiel's gloss on Rabbi Menachem Mendel Schneerson's (1902–94) gloss on Rabbi Shmuel Schneerson's (1834–82) Torah commentary.

metaphor. "Like an eagle awakens its nest, hovering over its young, He spread his wings and took him, carried him on His pinions" (Deut 32:11). In what way, they ask, is God "like" an eagle? An eagle flies high, but God is higher. Still, when speaking about God, what does "high" even mean? God is not in physical space. Actually, God is not really in mental space, either. We refer to God with various names, but really God is beyond all names. We speak of God's activity with various images, but none are literally accurate. One key Kabbalistic image comes from the creation story. Because God's first creation is light, Kabbalists often describe creation as an emanation of divine light. Divine energy flows first as spiritual light. Then, it takes conceptual form as intellectual light. Next, it moves in us as emotional light. Finally, it appears in its densest, most easily grasped form as physical light. Still, God flies even higher than spiritual light.[15] But, through emanation, God awakens us, the nestlings, so that we might direct our awareness up the spiritual ladder. God carries us on divine wings, so to speak.

In my own experience, that is exactly what a mystical experience can feel like—as if God has lifted you to the highest vantage point. Suddenly, you can see the big picture, like eagles, condors, and griffin vultures do. A new map, a clearer perception, a truer structure emerge. A few years ago, I was lifted in this way.

I was visiting New York, my home town, for a weekend psychology course on Cultural Complexes.[16] The teacher wanted us to explore an American complex. So, she took us on a field trip to the 9/11 Memorial. The museum sits where the World Trade Center once did, before the terrorist attack destroyed it and left 3,000 people dead. Tour guides, all local volunteers, share stories about their own experience on September 11, 2001.

Our tour guide was George, whose brother John died in the attack. John was a New York City police sergeant, and a first responder to the crisis. Our tour guide George described his terrible day of not knowing his brother's fate. At 11:00 pm, George's anxiety ended and his grief began. He received a call confirming

---

15. Steinsaltz, *Thirteen Petalled Rose*, 1–26.

16. Taught by Selig, author of *Integration*.

that his beloved brother had died. George invited us to ask him questions, but I didn't ask any. I just stood there, kind of dazed. Because my story is exactly the same as George's, with one exception. At 5:00 pm, I received a call confirming that my younger brother, also a police sergeant, was alive. My feelings from that day came back and overwhelmed me. I felt like I was hovering over an abyss again. The afternoon class, a workshop on grief poetry, did not ground me. My class notes were all about my other brother, my older brother, who died when he was a child.

In the evening, I returned to the home of my younger, living brother, where I stay when I'm in New York. I told him about our class field trip. For the first time, he spoke openly to me about the chaos he saw, as a police officer at Ground Zero on 9/11. For the first time, I understood why he had been so quiet about it. It wasn't just the emotional horror of 3,000 disasters happening all at once. There was a practical dimension, too. To deal with the magnitude of the emergency, the first responders had to improvise. Everything was insane.

Then, on the flight home to Vancouver, I had a mystical experience.

As I took my seat on the airplane, the man next to me put on giant headphones. He then actively avoided noticing me for four and a half hours. This bothered me. He had his reasons for wanting to be alone and they had nothing to do with me. Still, what he did sparked something for me. Despite the walls he put up, we were not actually separate. His thoughts, feelings, and actions affected me.

And I saw:

His psyche is inside him, and also outside of him.
Consciousness is both inside and outside each of us.
To imagine my consciousness centered in my body, as I usually do, is an illusion.
The source of experience lies beyond my body, brain, or mind.
What I am, what we are, is not bounded by our bodies.

Of course there is life after death, because the source of life does not die.

My old view of an "I" centered within me and generated by my brain is a false product of unclear thinking.

Just as gossip makes it hard to see people truly, so the conventions of language and dogmas of science make it hard to see myself truly.

To see clearly, I have to lift veils of opinion over and over again.

During this time, I was not at all "out of it." I sat in my seat, typed a report on my laptop, entertained someone's bored baby, walked through the airport, and endured the chaotic crush at baggage claim. I just did it all with a beatific smile on my face. Many people smiled back, delighted to be lifted for a moment out of their traveler's stress.[17]

Gradually, over the next two days, I floated down into everyday consciousness. And I reflected on my experience. In a way, it was paradoxical. On the one hand, psychology, philosophy, and religion seemed obviously false. They were only cultural constructs that block the truth. Cultural complexes, if you will, that ensnare us humans. On the other hand, studying Kabbalah obviously shaped my experience. For me, the theory of divine emanation came to life. For five hours, my attention focused fully on the spiritual realm. I soared past all intellectual concepts. Even at their best, it seemed, the concepts could only be partial metaphors. At their worst, they might be mistakes and lies. Mere images that no one who has soared could ever take too literally.

Winged Kingdom

Yet sometimes, I do take the Bible's animal metaphors literally. Most likely, biblical narratives were originally oral stories. Ancient oral stories belonged to specific groups of people.[18] Thus, they

17. Duhan-Kaplan, "Vibration of the Other," 124.
18. Aldred, "Resurrection of Story," 35.

spoke to specific audiences about familiar places.[19] Storytellers wove well-known local animals into their tales. So, if I want to know what they meant to say, I have to learn about those animals. In other words, I really do read looking for the author's original intent. But, at other times, I simply allow the metaphors to redirect my perception. A flash of insight shows up, and I see something anew—not necessarily something in the text. This approach honors my response as a reader, whatever it may be.[20]

The metaphor of God as an eagle has pointed my attention in new directions. Soaring from a new vantage point, I see things differently. Now, when I read the creation story, I sometimes picture the spiritual mother of the world, hovering over her incubating egg. This winged mother might have a special kinship with her winged babies. She might share a special spark of divinity with them. So, I now read other sections of the Tanakh differently, scanning for inter-textual clues about special winged creatures. I've noticed Isaiah's and Ezekiel's visions of winged beings in the heavenly temple, of course (Isa 6:1–13; Ezek 1:1–28). But I've also noticed some subtler allusions to bees and hornets, God's winged helpers.

For example, the Book of Judges suggests that bees and hornets both work for God. But the bee's work is more helpful to humans. Judges starts its history with the best leaders, who are like bees, and ends with the worst, who are like hornets. The name of the early judge and prophet Deborah means "bee." Like a bee, she uses her sting only for defense. She leads her people in a single defensive war, and then keeps the peace for forty years (Judg 4:1—5:31). But the last Judge, Samson, is more like a hornet (Judg 13:2—16:31). He comes from the town of *Tzorah,* which is spelled with the same letters as *tzirah,* hornet. Samson, angry and aggressive, even acts a bit like a hornet when he raids a beehive. He sticks his hand right in and takes the honey!

But my new perceptions also take me beyond the text. I've looked at bees, hornets, and wasps with a new curiosity. What if

19. Deloria, *God is Red,* 133–47.
20. Eagleton, *Literary Theory,* 47–79.

they reflect God's image in a special way? And the more carefully I've looked, the more these insects have looked back at me.

One summer day, I was at my usual place, the Grind Café on Main Street. I sat near the window, trying to get some writing done. But I got distracted by a loud buzzing. A bald-faced hornet was trying to get back outside. It flew, rested, flew, rested, and then crawled down the side of the table. This hornet was large. About ¾ of an inch long, with a black armored body, and a clownish white face. Normally I avoid hornets, but I had just read that some wild hornets pollinate flowers and eat aggressive yellowjackets.

So, I leaned over the edge of the table and I looked directly into the hornet's face. And I said, "Hi, beautiful! The window isn't safe. Here, climb on my notebook." Immediately the hornet crawled onto the table and made a beeline (so to speak) for the notebook. Then, it settled on the middle of a page and waited. At that time, I didn't know much about bald-faced hornets. So I said, "I don't know where you live. You'll have to tell me." I carried the notebook outdoors, to the nearest quiet street. I showed the hornet a flower. Not interested. Grass. Not interested. Soil. Nope. Finally, I brought the notebook to a tree trunk. "Yes, that's right!" the hornet said—in body language. It walked off the notebook and quickly climbed the tree. Honestly, I felt myself brought to a deeper life through contact with this alien intelligence.

Only a day later, a potter wasp got trapped under a glass tabletop on our deck. Potter wasps are slender, elegant, and usually calm. But this wasp was agitated. She buzzed loudly, flying up at the translucent table top over and over. However, the only route out was down. For just an instant, I focused my attention on her and gestured, moving my arm downwards. Immediately she flew down and out to freedom. I felt so pleased for her, but my husband was just puzzled. "You're so weird," he said—to me. But then I spoke with a bee biologist who said, "Of course you communicated with gestures! That's how wasps and bees speak to each other."[21]

Then, I began to notice the ingenuity of yellowjacket wasps. Generally, I avoid yellowjackets, who have stung me more than

21. Mark Winston, author of *Bee Time*.

once. But I forgot my caution the day I noticed a lone yellowjacket trying to solve a problem. She had found an orb-shaped spider's web with a little bit of hanging food wrapped in spidery silk. Her goal was to steal it without getting caught in the web. She tried several times, but couldn't knock the food down.

Another wasp came by, clearly a colleague from the same hive. They had a little meeting, wasp style, of course, dancing around in a perfect circle. Now the colleague understood the situation and was up to date on the unsuccessful attempts. So, she approached the web from a different angle. Still, no success. Again, the two wasps danced to debrief, analyze, and plan. But still, no success. During the third circle dance, the spider wisely fled. So, the wasps decided to do something bold. They approached a stick lying next to the web. One wasp grasped it with her feet, vibrated her wings, and lifted it a millimeter off the ground. But it was just too heavy for her to carry. At that moment, I was called away. Did they succeed in lifting the tool together, then knock down the food and feast? I hope so!

The next day, I looked for accessible articles on tool use among social insects. One promising abstract asked, "Is tool use in social insects a sign of intelligence?" But, in the end, the author said no. It is not intelligence, just a way to more effectively solve problems.[22] Oh no, I thought, this is the same question I wrestled with as a teen. In humans, effective problem-solving is a sign of intelligence. But, in insects it is not? Surely the dogmas of science have blocked this researcher's true perception. But, maybe one day, the eagle God will lift him up, too.

22. Pierce, "Review of Tool Use in Insects," 103.

Locust

Warning in the Mirror

AMONG GOD'S INSECT HELPERS, locusts are the best-known soldiers. Biblical writers knew that grasshoppers, under stress, turn into locusts. So, they understood that locusts are an excellent metaphor for human beings. We, too, change under stress. Sometimes, this helps us mobilize against oppression. But, sometimes we turn on ourselves. And then we have to find our way back to right living.

Biblical Background: From Grasshopper to Locust

In conversational English, the definitions of "locust" and "grasshopper" are flexible. So I have learned as I spoke with friends about my adventures with orthoptera. I've been bitten by a confused lubber and surprised by a Carolina locust. I've communed mystically with an American bird nymph and fed my pet toads commercial crickets, seen two-striped grasshoppers feasting on fields, and found camel-backs in my basement. Friends nod and tell their own stories, calling the critters "locusts," "grasshoppers," "katydids," or "crickets," depending on their regional dialect.

But biblical writers seem to have a specific species in mind: a solitary desert grasshopper that transforms, at God's command, into a swarming locust. They use their distinct terms for "grasshopper" and "locust" quite precisely. But each time they speak of a peaceful "grasshopper," they hint at its potential transformation into a wild, destructive force. Even more ominously, they hint that humans, too, have this terrible promise.

The most common Hebrew word for grasshopper, *khagav*, is related to the Arabic root *hibabun*, "that which veils, conceals, hides."[1] Perhaps the species name hints that its simple life conceals a more threatening side: its transformation into *arbeh*, the swarming locust. *Arbeh* probably comes from the Hebrew root *rav*, many. But, read as an anagram, the word tells the story of this insect's life cycle. Rearrange its four letters, *aleph, resh, bet, hey*, and learn. Solitary grasshoppers travel to the well, *be'erah*. That's spelled *bet, aleph, resh, hey*. There, God says, "I will multiply them, *arbeh* them, spelled *aleph, resh, bet, hay*. Then, they become something new that God created, *barah Hashem*—spelled *bet, resh, aleph, hey*.

Science Catches Up: Locust Swarms

Modern scientists have only recently recovered this ancient knowledge about grasshopper biology. For years, they tried to understand where *schistocerca gregaria*, desert locusts, go between swarms. Biologists searched for locust colonies at rest, but never found any. Still, they were positive locusts did not simply pop in and out of existence. Finally, in 1921, entomologist Boris Uvarov figured it out. Between plagues, locusts live as solitary grasshoppers. But, when conditions demand it, the grasshoppers physically transform into locusts.[2]

Normally, grasshoppers prefer personal space and avoid touching other grasshoppers. Still, when desert drought gets extreme, they congregate around the few moist patches left. Eventually the area gets so crowded that the grasshoppers can't move without rubbing up against one another. So, the grasshoppers adapt. Their brain chemistry changes. Their serotonin levels rise.

---

1. *BDB (Brown Driver Briggs)*, 290.
2. Dillard, *Pilgrim at Tinker Creek*, 209–11.

Their bodies harden. They eat more. Mate more. Develop a group mind. And they fly off together in search of food.

Once they've swarmed, nothing can stand in their way. A swarm is densely packed with as many as 80 million locusts per half square mile.[3] In one day, these 80 million locusts can eat enough to feed 35,000 people.[4] But rarely is a cloud of locusts as small as half a mile. Locust swarms as big as 460 square miles in size have been observed. And a swarm this size can eat the daily ration for 32 billion people. So, when a swarm strips a field, it moves right on to the next one, even if it has to fly 80 miles across a sea to find it.[5]

If you farm in Egypt or Israel today, you may be lucky. Military satellites can detect the beginning of a locust swarm. Then, the ministry of agriculture can destroy the insects before too many emerge. But, if you are a small farmer farther south in Africa, dependent on a local economy, your food supply for the year may be stolen by the swarm.[6] Often, the swarm is the third blow in a series of disasters. First comes the drought, stunting your crops. This same drought pushes the grasshoppers into the last few moist areas. Next comes the flood that drowns your meager crop. This same flood dumps enough water to sustain a growing locust colony. Finally, the locusts take flight, and consume what little you have left. Fortunately, a swarm does not reproduce itself forever.[7] When environmental conditions stabilize, and spacious grasshopper habitats come available, the metamorphosis stops.

Isaiah: Locusts are God's Messengers

That is the biblical locust/grasshopper: a species on the edge of a dual life. Thus, it makes a powerful metaphor. In this densely

3. Holland, "Locusts Eat the Crops of Madagascar."

4. Emily Tyee quoted in Business Insider, "Swarms of Locusts are Invading East Africa."

5. National Geographic, "Locusts."

6. Ian Couzin in Holland, "Locusts Eat the Crops of Madagascar."

7. Hojun Song, quoted in Kaufman, "How This Big Locust Plague Will End."

packed oracle, the prophet Isaiah hints at the messages a meta-phorical locust carries.

> Don't you get it? . . . God dwells above the circle *(khug)* of the earth, and those who dwell on earth are like grass-hoppers *(khagavim)*. . . . God brings princes to naught, and makes the rulers of the earth as nothing. Scarcely are they planted, scarcely sown, when God blows upon them, and they wither. . . . Lift up your eyes on high and see: Who created these? The One who brings out their host and counts them, calling them all by name. Because God is great in strength, mighty in power, not one fails to show up. (Isa 40:21–24)

With a play on words, Isaiah contrasts God, the heavenly dweller, with human earth-dwellers. God looks down from above the *khug*, the horizon that circles the earth. To God, the little crea-tures encircled within the *khug* are like *khagavim*. A grasshopper, two inches long, looks tiny to a human; so imagine how tiny we look to God.

Some humans forget how small a role they play in God's vast universe. They become tyrants, lording it over creation, seeing the world as a resource for their own enrichment. They establish dynasties to keep wealth within their families. But, in God's eyes, these dynasties are as short-lived as they are small. Like annual crops, they sprout for a season, then wither and die.

God can cut short even that brief span. To make it happen, God calls on the *khagavim,* the tiniest ones, and they respond. These *khagavim* may be literal grasshoppers, rising up in a giant locust swarm. Together, they devour the tyrant's fields, upending the tyrant's cruel self-serving economy. Thus they undermine the structures the tyrant tried to plant. The locusts may look to us like a mindless horde; but in God's eyes, they are valued individuals, loyal to a collective mission. No wonder locusts appear as one of the plagues in the exodus story! God sends them, along with the other plagues, to bring spiritual awareness to the arrogant, exploit-ative Pharaoh.[8]

8. Leibowitz, *New Studies in Shemot Exodus*, 170–77.

But the *khagavim*, the tiny earth dwellers that God mobilizes, might sometimes be human armies. Eventually, Isaiah hints, the oppressed will rise up. Tyrants might discount them as nothing, but in God's eyes, they count.

Joel: Desolation after Locust Invasion

Like locusts, humans also have a double life. Ideally, we live at peace, but tyrants drive us to war. This, suggests the prophet Joel, is a timeless feature of human society. He explores it in his short, unusual book. Joel's book is styled as a series of prophetic oracles to a post-exilic (after 586 BCE) community in Judah. But the book has no time stamp, and no correlation with specific historical events. Instead, it drops you right into an archetypal story.

The prophet Joel stands before a community devastated by a locust plague. Joel, a master of comfort, acknowledges the ruin. The locust plague, he says, is like an invading army (Joel 2:4–11).[9] The locusts look like horses, sound like chariots, rush like warriors, and enter like thieves (Joel 2:4–9). They terrify the livestock and shatter human endeavor. Even their babies are vicious; every instar (developmental form) assaults the food supply (Joel 1:4).[10]

Then, Joel calls the people into community. "Wake up drunkards!" he says, "This is no time to self-medicate with wine! Get back to work, priests, and lead us in rituals of lament and healing! Because, after trauma, God will restore the community."

Finally, Joel seems to change the subject. It's as if he knows the locusts are only his community's latest problem. Even before the swarm came, they were already beaten down by imperial incursions. No wonder locusts brought back memories of horses, chariots, warriors, and thieves. Armies had already invaded, looted, and exiled the people of Judah.

So, Joel says, God will eventually judge these invaders. In fact, Judah will retaliate, capturing their old enemies, and selling them

9. Simkins, "God, History, and the Natural World in the Book of Joel"; Assis, "Structure and Meaning of the Locust Plague Oracles in Joel 1:2—2:17."

10. Yamauchi, "Ancient Ecologies and the Biblical Perspective."

into slavery. When the time comes, Joel says, farmers must fight on God's side. Joel calls on them to "beat your plowshares into swords and your pruning hooks into spears"—inverting Isaiah's famous oracle of peace (Joel 4:10). "Swing the sickle, for the crop is ripe!" Joel says (Joel 4:13). But this harvest will be the dead bodies of foes. If I hold Isaiah in mind, I understand: when God calls, the oppressed of Judah will swarm like locusts. They will strip every bit of life from their oppressors, reducing them to nothing. And then, mission accomplished, they will calm down, returning to their grasshopper life.

Numbers: Our Human Grasshopper-Locust Life Cycle

Biblical writers understand the locust life cycle itself, along with the political and psychological cycles of war and peace. But sometimes biblical characters understand neither. The effect can be funny, ironic, chilling—or even all three at once. We see this in the Book of Numbers, for example. Moses sends twelve scouts to tour the land of Canaan. When they return, they file their report before the people (Num 13:1—14:39).

"Look at this giant fruit that grows there!" the scouts say. "You need two people just to carry a cluster of grapes."

"But," they add, "the people who live there are gigantic. Next to them, we feel like grasshoppers. And that's how we looked to them!"

One scout wants to go back to conquer the land. "We can do it!"

Ten scouts disagree. "The place will eat us."

The Israelites wail and cry. They scream at Moses and Aaron for dragging them out of Egypt, and announce that they are going back. When Joshua tries to intervene, the mob picks up stones and prepares to attack. So, God intervenes. The divine presence appears to everyone. And God tells Moses that this generation is not fit to conquer the land. But, in forty years, their children and grandchildren will be ready.

There it is: funny, ironic, and chilling. The story is funny, because the scouts, who do not enjoy feeling like insects, seem to act just as social insects might. They sound just like ants, for example, reporting to the colony about their visit to a kitchen filled with wonderful giant fruit and angry giant humans.

But, as the biblical story unfolds, the comedy opens into a more complex irony.[11] To see it, we read intertextually, that is, in conversation with other biblical texts. In ironic speech, a person uses words to mean their exact opposite. Here, the scouts unwittingly use ironic speech when they say they look to the locals like tiny, weak grasshoppers. Forty years later, they learn that the locals actually see them as a powerful horde of locusts. King Balak of Moab, who fears the Israelite army, says, "They will lick up everything around us!" They will "hide the land from view" (Num 22:4–5), just as the plague of locusts in the exodus story "hid the land from view" (Exod 10:15). As readers, we can enjoy the image of timid grasshopper parents raising fearsome locust children. Or cheer on the Israelites as they grow into their own surprising power. We can explore our own existential questions about faith, fear, and imagination.

But the story holds another level of irony, this one more chilling. Those who receive the scouts' report cannot imagine themselves as a fierce locust swarm. But, in fact, they act like one. After wandering through desert droughts, they hear a story of abundant harvests. But the orchards are owned by giants, and the image terrifies them. So, afraid and angry, they transmute into a mob. They pick up weapons and threaten to use them. In fact, they are quite ready to, as Joel says, rush like warriors and shatter human communities. As it turns out, God, Moses, and Joshua want them to develop more discipline. But they already have the personality traits that can be moved to violence. When conditions are right, they will swarm.

Eventually, they will retreat to their peaceful grasshopper life. But here the insect-to-human analogy breaks down. Unlike grasshoppers, humans are not solitary; we live in community.

11. Lerner, "Timid Grasshoppers and Fierce Locusts."

Collectively, we create civic peace. Our kind of grasshopper life requires community ritual, limits on inequality, and legal accountability. At least, that is what Moses teaches.

Afterthoughts: Joel Today

This chapter's harsh view of human nature hits too close to home. It's impossible not to see analogies with modern times. For example, today modern imperial forces, i.e., transnational corporations, scour the globe for resources.[12] Sometimes they leave devastation and drought.[13] They drive the use of fossil fuels, increasing greenhouse gases and raising global temperatures. The earth's turbulent atmosphere generates more storms. Wild swings between drought and flood birth more locust swarms. But tyrants do not get the message; instead, small farmers bear the brunt.

Meanwhile, the corporate quest for profit continues,[14] with war as a tool. Wars win control of resources, subjugate populations, reinforce the arms industry, generate redevelopment contracts. For some industries, and the governments that support them, the cruelty of war becomes a permanent way of life.[15] Thus, people come to believe that only more violence can end the cycle. They pray for the apocalyptic end Joel describes.[16]

But, as a critical reader of Joel, I believe that the harvest of war is death. People cannot live forever in our swarming locust frenzy. Our fields can only bear so much stripping. There is, as Moses teaches, a time to strengthen institutions of equality, accountability, and peace. And maybe that time is now.

12. Korten, *When Corporations Rule the World*, Kindle.

13. Hedges and Sacco, *Days of Destruction, Days of Revolt*, Kindle.

14. Joel Bakan, *The Corporation*.

15. Hedges, *Empire of Illusion*, Kindle.

16. Juergensmeyer, *Terror in the Mind of God*, 82–203.

Wolf and Lamb Together

Peace Is Possible

INTERSPECIES FRIENDSHIPS ARE REALLY not unusual. We see them up close, between farm animals and pets. Occasionally, we see them where wild spaces touch human communities. My cat Keely, for example, used to play hide and seek with a squirrel. They became friends on the deck outside our back door; I did not introduce them. Koi-cat protected Buddy the love bird's cage from an interloping feline neighbor. Though I never let Koi and Buddy roam freely together, they developed a mutual respect. Buddy, unruffled, let Koi sleep on a towel atop his cage. Interspecies co-existence is even more unremarkable. Most animals don't spend all their time eating each other. Instead, they move through their environments, making space for other creatures. Really, animal friendships aren't newsworthy at all.

Why, then, are animal friendship stories so popular?[1] Here's one thought: they're fables, stories about human life. Some of them symbolically describe ideal communities. Here is one example, a childhood favorite of mine. It's the "Bremen Town Musicians," a fairy tale collected by the Brothers Grimm. A donkey, dog, cat, and rooster have worked hard on farms for years. But, now that they are elderly, and ready to retire, their human masters are done with them. Rather than feed and care for them, the masters plan to kill them. So they leave their farms together, expecting they'll figure

---

1. Goode, "Learning from Animal Friendships."

out how to support each other. Turns out people find this unlikely gang of marginal types quite scary. One night, they stand outside a house, thinking they will sing for their supper. But, when they sing together, each in their native tongue, the criminal gang inside flees in terror. The "musicians" move into the house, feasting as friends until the end of their days.[2] What a beautiful, all-too-human story about redemption from the cruel life of a powerless laborer! You work for a boss who doesn't see you as family but only as a commodity. But, you band together with other workers, chase away the criminals, and live frugally together, using only what you need.

Remember the children's book *Charlotte's Web* by E. B. White? A group of barnyard friends organizes to save the life of one young pig. A spider, with the help of a rat, convinces the humans that the piglet is extraordinary. Really, there is nothing special about this piglet except that someone loves him. But Charlotte, the spider who leads the effort, is quite skilled. Still, her goals are modest: save one pig, don't challenge the system. She does what she can and dies satisfied, knowing she has made a difference.[3] Charlotte represents many humans who work to save others. We create a poster child; call attention to a cause; and do some local good in a difficult world. And we yearn to believe, as Charlotte does, that it's enough.

So, I want to close with a biblical fable about animal friendship. This fable brings hope—real hope. Its vision of peace looks like a fairy tale. But, I will argue, this peace can and has come to be. Sustaining it takes work, of course, but the fable tells us exactly what to do.

The Wolf and the Lamb

This parable is the prophet Isaiah's oracle about the wolf and the lamb. Most interpreters read it as a visionary fable about human life. According to the Bible, Isaiah speaks into a particular political crisis. It's the eighth century BCE, and prophet Isaiah son of Amoz

2. *Grimm's Fairy Tales*, "Bremen Town Musicians," Kindle.

3. White, *Charlotte's Web*.

is a spiritual advisor to kings of Judah.[4] Times are bad, Isaiah says. Local leaders prioritize their own wealth over community care. The Assyrian empire threatens to invade. It's time for local leaders to take responsibility, repent, and change. When they do, Assyrian aggressors will lose their influence and God will dissolve the Assyrian empire (Isa 10:12). Then, a righteous Israelite king, committed to equity and justice, will come to power (Isa 11:1–5).

And then, society will be transformed. Isaiah says:

> A wolf shall visit with a lamb, a leopard lie down with a kid. A calf, young lion, and fatling together, and a little child shall guide them. A cow and bear shall graze; their young lie down together. And a lion, like an ox, shall eat straw. A baby shall play over a viper's hole; and over an adder's fang, a toddler shall extend its hand. No one will do evil or destroy, anywhere on My holy mountain. For the land shall be filled with knowledge of the YHWH as water covers the sea. (Isa 11:6–9)

Classical commentators agree: this is a vision of an ideal human community. But they disagree on how it will come about. Does Isaiah imagine political, ethical, or spiritual change? Will it be a new form of human life, or a return to a golden age? Can leaders bring it about, or must everyone participate?

Rabbi Meir Wisser (a.k.a. the Malbim, 1809–79) says Isaiah offers a fable about a future political change. The lion represents Babylon and Assyria. Kings of both those nations used lions as symbols of their royal power.[5] One day, the predatory empires won't consume little nations. Instead, they will seek peace and share resources.

But, says Rabbi David Kimchi (a.k.a. the Radak, 1160–1235), this is not just a possible future vision. Instead, it reinstates primordial realities. Long ago, Kimchi says, animal nature was nonviolent. In the Garden of Eden, species did not prey on one another. And on Noah's Ark, they adapted to close, peaceful living. They had to! In Eden, God only created a few of each species. And,

---

4. Brettler, *How to Read the Jewish Bible*, Kindle.

5. Malbim on Daniel 7:4.

on the Ark, God only rescued a few of each. So, if predators had eaten meat, their prey would have quickly become extinct. And then the predators themselves would have starved to death.[6] In human communities, predators are the opportunistic wealthy, and prey are the poor. This is an unsustainable pattern. To break it, we must take inspiration from animals at their best.

From these animals, suggests Isaac Abarbanel (1437–1508), we will learn to break the patterns of aggression involved in hunting and killing.[7] Like them, says Rabbi Nachman of Breslov (1772–1810), we will have compassion for one another, and know that God's love flows to all creatures.[8] We will know not to start violent fights over differences of opinion. Our wisdom, suggests Maimonides (1135–1204), will dissolve enmities as entrenched as wolf and lamb, human and snake.[9]

Developing Peace through Friendship: A Poetic Analysis

But it won't happen automatically—at least, that's my view. God may wave a magic wand, but that can only raise spiritual awareness and start the change. Humans will have to do most of the work. Fortunately, Isaiah lays out a plan. Citizens freed from oppression don't seek revenge. Instead, they turn away from that destructive impulse, and educate youth in peaceful values. Mothers raise their children with a diverse set of friends. Then, the community recognizes the power of pacifism. New generations of children grow up without trauma. And finally, "no evil will be done."

Isaiah's plan is expressed in animal metaphors. Once we analyze the oracle's poetic form, it's easy to see the plan. Isaiah 11:6–9 is a typical unit of biblical poetry. Unlike modern English poetry, its key features are not rhyme or meter. Instead, it places

---

6. Radak on Isaiah 11:6.

7. Abarbanel on Isaiah 11:8.

8. Reb Nachman of Breslov, *Likutei Moharan*, 33:46; 56:6:2; 14:11:3.

9. Maimonides, *Guide for the Perplexed*, 3:11.

metaphors in relationship to one another. The typical structure of each verse is a kind of parallelism. The first part of the verse presents a metaphor. Then the second part presents a similar metaphor that amplifies, extends, or comments on the first.[10] Often there's a second level of metaphorical play, too, where whole verses comment on each other. Some metaphors might only make sense to Isaiah's contemporaries. But others are based on literary hints that thread through the Bible. And these will help us learn from Isaiah's fable.

Power Dynamics Flip

How does biblical literature understand "wolf" and "lamb"? Both can represent human beings. The wolf is violent; the lamb is passive. When Jacob is on his deathbed, he shares visions of his sons' future lives. "Benjamin," he says, "is a ravenous wolf; in the morning he consumes the foe, and in the evening he divides the spoil" (Gen 49:27). But there's no story about Benjamin doing violence. So medieval commentator Rashi points to a story where descendants of Benjamin rape, kill, and kidnap (Judg 19–21).[11] They are the "ravenous wolves," the violent human aggressors.

Sheep sometimes represent the humans in God's flock (see, for example, the sheep chapter).[12] But, lambs themselves may have a different connotation. Torah often talks about lambs as property[13] or food offerings.[14] The Hebrew word for lamb, *keves*, is related to the Hebrew words for conquer, subdue, and take into bondage. So, the lambs, here, are people of defeated nations. And yet, in Isaiah's oracle, the lambs control the land. Power dynamics flip; both *who* rules and *how* change. The lambs are peaceful; they

---

10. Berlin, "Reading Biblical Poetry."

11. *Mikraot Gedolot*, Rashi on Genesis 49:27.

12. See, for example, Ezek 34, Ps 23.

13. See, for example, Gen 30:32, 1 Sam 17:34.

14. See, for example, Lev 1–5.

govern without a policy of revenge. Graciously and with mercy, they allow the wolves to sojourn as guests.

Of course, you're skeptical. Such a radical change seems impossible. That's why Isaiah goes on to reassure us. The leopard can indeed lie down with the kid. Here, the young goat, a food animal and a commodity, may simply be a synonym for the lamb.[15] But the image of the leopard adds a new point. Elsewhere, the prophet Jeremiah asks, "Can a leopard change its spots?" (Jer 13:23) For Jeremiah, this is an ironic rhetorical question. He does not believe that evil people can ever learn to do good. *But Isaiah does.*

Children Learn a New Way

Isaiah seems to know that youth often join crowds, gangs, and militias. Sometimes they feel more powerful when they threaten others. But Isaiah believes that even teens and young adults can change; that's why he speaks explicitly of the young lion. In prophetic literature, the young lion roars loudly.[16] Bluster is its signature move. But that posture, Isaiah suggests, can be re-directed into a passion for peace. If, that is, mothers commit to raising their children differently. Fierce mothers will have to take the lead in teaching narratives of peace, not revenge.[17]

Here, those mothers are the cow and the bear. Cow, a feminine noun, obviously refers to a mother. In agricultural life, a cow is often a bereaved mother, whose children are sold or slaughtered. And bears in the Tanakh are usually mother bears, savagely seeking their missing cubs.[18] In Isaiah's vision, these two grieving mothers bond. They set aside their painful histories and, together, they seek a new way of living. They raise their children, different as they are, side by side, as friends.

15. The kid appears as food in Gen 27:9; Exod 23:19; 34:26, Deut 14:21; as a gift or payment in Gen 38:20–23 and Judg 15:1; and as a source of garments in Gen 27:16.

16. Judg 14:5; Jer 2:15; 51:38; Amos 3:4; Zech 11:3; Ps 104:21.

17. See, for example, Ruddick, *Maternal Thinking.*

18. 2 Sam 17:8; Prov 17:12; Hos 13:8.

Even the Fierce Can Change

With good education, Isaiah believes, even the fiercest natures can change. Take, for example, the ox and the lion. The biblical ox is a fearsome animal. Unrestrained, it can kill a human being or even another ox.[19] But, properly cared for, an ox can help humans grow and transport food. And the biblical lion, formidable as it is, can also be trained. For example, a lion on a mission from God can stand calmly next to a donkey.[20] With a little help from an angel, a lion can refuse to eat a prophet.[21]

And when the fiercest change, the innocent can be safe, even from accidental harm. When the viper, a.k.a. adder, waits to ambush its prey, it hopes to catch a rat or a lizard. But a human child, unaware of its surroundings, could surprise the viper. Then, the snake might respond with a defensive but deadly bite. So it is, Isaiah suggests, with human "snakes." That's what biblical poets call corrupt people who, for profit, pretend to be victims.[22] These wicked profiteers also lie in wait for their prey. But their schemes don't harm only the intended mark. They can also harm families, communities, and public institutions. But, when they are de-fanged, so to speak, through education, no more innocents will be harmed. And then, the next generation will grow up without trauma, ready to embrace an ideal vision.

Isaiah's Oracle Is Real: Indigenous-Settler Peace and Friendship Treaties

Can Isaiah's vision come true? According to American painter Edward Hicks (1780–1849), it can and it has—at some times and in some places. Hicks, a self-taught painter, was a Quaker minister in Pennsylvania. His life was filled with conflict—political, familial, church, and psychological. He worked through his conflicts by

19. Exod 21:28–32, 35–36.

20. 1 Kgs 20:36.

21. Dan 6:23.

22. Isa 59:5; Ps 58:5

painting Isaiah's animal oracle. Hicks painted more than fifty versions of this painting, which he called "The Peaceable Kingdom."[23] For Hicks, the animals could represent the dynamics in a soul, a family, a community, or even between two nations. He would paint the animals more or less at peace. It all depended on how the particular conflict was resolving.[24]

Edward Hicks, *Peaceable Kingdom*, c. 1834[25]

This version of "The Peaceable Kingdom" is one of my favorites. It hangs on the wall in my office, in the Indigenous and Inter-Religious Studies program at the Vancouver School of Theology. In this painting, the animals relax very peaceably on a hill. In the Delaware river valley below, the American colonial leader William Penn and Chief Tamanend of the Lenape Nation agree to the Shackamaxon Treaty of 1683. Some say Hicks' painting idealizes

23. Hicks, *A Peaceable Season.*

24. Cotter, "Finding Endless Conflict Hidden in a Peaceable Kingdom."

25 Courtesy National Gallery of Art, Washington.

colonial history.[26] But I think it documents the power of treaty, as the Shackamaxon treaty mostly kept the local peace for seventy years.

The Shackamaxon treaty is documented in a Lenape wampum belt. Ninety years later, artist Benjamin West developed the belt's images into a painting that inspired Hicks' version.[27] But the details of the treaty are lost. Some say there was a written agreement, but Penn's sons later destroyed it to further their business interests.[28] But, more likely, the treaty was an oral agreement based in ceremony.[29] The treaty probably included few details, as it was not modelled on a business contract, but on a treaty of peace and friendship.

A treaty, says Cree theologian Raymond Aldred, is an "agreement to live in a harmonious way upon this place."[30] He sees a treaty as a ceremony for becoming relatives. His favorite illustration is Black Elk's story of the Sioux and Ree creating a ceremony to integrate their nations and share their corn.[31] The early "Peace and Friendship Treaties" are also good examples of such agreements. These treaties were affirmed by the Mi'kmaq, Maliseet, and Passamaquoddy First Nations and representatives of Great Britain. The first one was signed in 1726, in the region now called Nova Scotia. There, the Mi'kmaq hoped to fish without interference from British settlers, and Great Britain hoped to start a lasting alliance. To meet both sets of needs, a working group drafted two documents, with reciprocal promises for sharing the land. The First Nations agreed not to molest the British in their settlements. The British agreed not to molest the local communities as they fished, hunted, and planted.[32] During the ratification ceremony, both sides agreed

26. Chan and Metzler, "Lions and Leopards and Bears, O My."

27. Newman, "The Treaty of Shackamaxon"; Historical Society of Pennsylvania, "Wampum Belt."

28. Jennings, *The Invasion of America*.

29. Chang, Wu, Forde, and Kim, "Penn's Treaty with the Lenape."

30. Aldred and Duhan-Kaplan, *Spirit of Reconciliation*, 10.

31. Brown, *The Sacred Pipe*, 101–15.

32. Wicken, "Fact Sheet on Peace and Friendship Treaties."

not to settle disputes by taking revenge.[33] Later treaties reaffirmed the promises and provisions of the first treaty, and added specific economic agreements that supported the evolving relationship.[34]

The Peace and Friendship treaties are quite different from nineteenth-century treaties mandating the surrender of land to the Canadian government.[35] As Mi'kmaw educator Marie Battiste writes:

> The treaties are about sharing what the Mi'kmaq had in abundance and the idea of equal opportunity through trade and respecting human rights. They are not about military conquest, "might makes right," or other theories leading to injustice.[36]

The treaties are an expression, I might say, of people committed to an ethic like the one Isaiah describes. Like the wolf and the lamb, they resist conquest and revenge. They welcome one another as fellow residents. Like the lion and the ox who share a food source, they rise to the opportunity for peace. And, like the bear and the cow, they understand that the relationship must be renewed in every generation. In other words, Isaiah's oracle is not just a metaphorical gateway to hope. It also resonates with successful acts of civic friendship. And, in that, we should find real hope.

33. Palmater "My Tribe, My Heirs and Their Heirs Forever."
34. Brown and Wicken, "Interpreting the Treaties."
35. Wicken, "Fact Sheet on Peace and Friendship Treaties."
36. Battiste, *Living Treaties: Narrating Mi'kmaw Treaty Relations.*

Bibliography

Abarbanel, Isaac. *Commentary on Isaiah.* Sefaria. https://www.sefaria.org/ Abarbanel_on_Isaiah?lang=en/.

Abram, David. *Becoming Animal: An Earthly Cosmology.* New York: Vintage, 2010. Kindle.

———. *The Spell of the Sensuous: Perception and Language in a More-Than-Human World.* New York: Vintage, 1997.

Aldred, Ray. "The Resurrection of Story." *William Carey International Development Journal* 3.2 (2014) 32–38.

Aldred, Ray, and Laura Duhan-Kaplan, eds. *Spirit of Reconciliation.* Toronto: Canadian Race Relations Foundation, 2020.

Almalech, Money. "Biblical Donkey." In *Proceedings of the World Congress of the International Association for Semiotic Studies,* 816–27. Sofia, Bulgaria: New Bulgarian University Press, 2014.

Alter, Robert. *The Art of Biblical Narrative.* New York: Basic, 2011. Kindle.

Anderson, Kim. *Life Stages and Native Women.* Winnipeg: University of Manitoba Press, 2011.

Andrews, Ted. *Animal-Wise: Understanding the Language of Animal Messengers and Companions.* Jackson, TN: Dragonhawk, 2009.

Assis, Elie. "The Structure and Meaning of the Locust Plague Oracles in Joel 1:2—2:17." *Zeitschrift für die alttestamentliche Wissenschaft* 122.3 (2010) 401–16.

Bakan, Joel. *The Corporation: The Pathological Pursuit of Profit and Power.* New York: Free, 2004.

Battiste, Marie, ed. *Living Treaties: Narrating Mi'kmaw Treaty Relations.* Sydney, NS: Cape Breton University Press, 2016. Kindle.

Bedard, Stephen J. "Did Jesus Ride Two Donkeys into Jerusalem?" *Stephenjbedard.com,* March 9, 2016. http://www.stephenjbedard. com/2016/03/19/did-jesus-ride-two-donkeys-into-jerusalem/.

Berlin, Adele. "Reading Biblical Poetry." In *The Jewish Study Bible,* edited by Adele Berlin and Marc Zvi Brettler, 2097–2104. Oxford: Oxford University Press, 2004.

Black, Max. *Models and Metaphors.* Ithaca, NY: Cornell University Press, 1962.

————. "More about Metaphor." In *Metaphor and Thought*, edited by Andrew Ortony, 19–43. Cambridge: Cambridge University Press, 1979.

Blue, Debbie. *Consider the Birds: A Provocative Guide to Birds of the Bible*. Nashville, TN: United Methodist, 2013.

Bonaiuti, Ernesto, and Giorgio La Piana. "The Genesis of St. Augustine's Idea of Original Sin." *Harvard Theological Review* 10.2 (1917) 159–75.

Boone, J. Allen. *Kinship with All Life*. San Francisco: Harper, 1954.

Brettler, Marc Zvi. *How to Read the Jewish Bible*. Philadelphia: Jewish Publication Society, 2005.

Brown, Douglas, and William Wicken. "Interpreting the Treaties." *Canada's History*, April 30, 2018. https://www.canadashistory.ca/explore/politics-law/interpreting-the-treaties.

Brown, Francis, S. R. Driver, and Charles A. Briggs. *A Hebrew and English Lexicon of the Old Testament*. New York: Houghton Mifflin, 1907. http://tmcdaniel.palmerseminary.edu/BDB.pdf/.

Brown, Joseph Epes. *The Sacred Pipe: Black Elk's Account of the Rites of the Oglala Sioux*. Norman, OK: University of Oklahoma Press, 2012.

Business Insider, "Swarms of Locusts are Invading East Africa and Destroying Crops." February 25, 2020. https://www.businessinsider.com/locusts-africa-kenya-farmers-crops-2020-2/.

Carasik, Michael, ed. *The Commentator's Bible: Leviticus*. Philadelphia: Jewish Publication Society, 2009.

Casas, Bartolomé de las, and Nigel Griffin. *A Short Account of the Destruction of the Indies*. New York: Penguin, 1992.

Chan, Michael J., and Maria Metzler. "Lions and Leopards and Bears, O My: Re-reading Isaiah 11:6–9 in Light of Comparative Iconographic and Literary Evidence." In *Image, Text, Exegesis: Iconographic Interpretation*, edited by Izaak J. de Hulster and Joel M. LeMon, 196–225. London: Bloomsbury, 2014.

Chang, Hannah, Jimmy Wu, Ben Forde, and Ari Kim. "The Legend of Penn's Treaty with the Lenape." *Haverford College Libraries*, 2017. http://ds.haverford.edu/penn-treaty-elm/essays/lenape/

Cherry, Shai. *Torah through Time*. Philadelphia: Jewish Publication Society, 2007. Kindle.

Cotter, Holland. "Finding Endless Conflict Hidden in a Peaceable Kingdom." *The New York Times*, June 16, 2000. https://www.nytimes.com/2000/06/16/arts/art-review-finding-endless-conflict-hidden-in-a-peaceable-kingdom.html/.

Cox, Brenda. *Conversations with an Eagle: The Story of a Remarkable Relationship*. Vancouver, BC: Greystone, 2002. Kindle.

Davis, Ellen F. *Scripture, Culture, and Agriculture: An Agrarian Reading of the Bible*. Cambridge: Cambridge University Press, 2008.

Dean, Dorothy. "Theology, Friendship, and the Human Animal." Lecture at the American Academy of Religion, December 10, 2020.

Deloria, Vine. *God Is Red: A Native View of Religion*. London: Fulcrum, 2003.

Dillard, Annie. *Pilgrim at Tinker Creek*. New York: HarperCollins, 2009. Kindle.

Douglas, Mary. *Leviticus as Literature*. New York: Oxford University Press, 1999.

Duhan-Kaplan, Laura. "The Blood of Life: The Hatat Offering and September 11, 2001." *Jewish Biblical Quarterly* 129 (2005) 47–52.

———. "Crows Are Nesting in Our Backyard!" *Sophia Street*, June 9, 2018. https://www.sophiastreet.com/2018/06/09/crows-nesting-backyard/.

———. "Edmund Husserl." In *The Great Thinkers A to Z*, edited by Julian Baggini, 122–24. New York: Continuum, 2003.

———. *The Infinity Inside: Jewish Spiritual Practice through a Multi-Faith Lens*. Boulder, CO: Albion-Andalus, 2019.

———. "Vibration of the Other: A Kabbalistic Ecumenism." In *Encountering the Other: Christian and Multifaith Perspectives*, edited by Laura Duhan-Kaplan and Harry O. Maier, 118–26. Eugene, OR: Pickwick, 2020.

Eagleton, Terry. *Literary Theory: An Introduction*. 2nd ed. Minneapolis: University of Minnesota Press, 1996.

Ehrlich, Paul R., David S. Dobkin, and Darryl Wheye. "Transporting Young." *Birds of Stanford*, 1988. https://web.stanford.edu/group/stanfordbirds/text/essays/Transporting_Young.html/.

Elior, Rachel. *The Three Temples: On the Emergence of Jewish Mysticism*. Oxford: Oxford University Press, 2005.

Elliot, Kyle, Jason Duffe, Sandi E. Lee, Pierre Mineau, and John Elliott. "Foraging Ecology of Bald Eagles at an Urban Landfill." *The Wilson Journal of Ornithology* 118 (September 2006) 380–90.

Feigelson, Mimi. "Wisdom: A Torah Study." Lecture at the ALEPH Kallah, July 2001.

Fishbane, Michael. "Ethics and Sacred Attunement." *The Journal of Religion* 93.4 (2013) 421–33.

Fleming, Daniel E. "Living by Livestock in Israel's Exodus: Explaining Origins over Distance." In *Israel's Exodus in Transdisciplinary Perspective: Text, Archaeology, Culture, and Geoscience*, edited by Thomas E. Levy, Thomas Schneider, and William H. C. Propp, 483–91. Heidelberg: Springer, 2015.

Frankel, David. "Datan and Abiram: A Rebellion of the Shepherds in the Land of Israel." *TheTorah.com*, 2016. https://thetorah.com/article/datan-and-abiram-a-rebellion-of-the-shepherds-in-the-land-of-israel/.

Goode, Erica. "Learning from Animal Friendships." *The New York Times*, January 27, 2015. https://www.nytimes.com/2015/01/27/science/so-happy-together.html/.

Gordon, William J. J. *The Metaphorical Way of Learning and Knowing*. Cambridge, MA: Porpoise, 1973.

Government of Canada. "Peace and Friendship Treaties." 2015. https://www.rcaanc-cirnac.gc.ca/eng/1100100028589/1539608999656/.

Green, Arthur. *Ehyeh: A Kabbalah for Tomorrow*. Woodstock, VT: Jewish Lights, 2003.

Grimm, Brothers. *Grimm's Fairy Tales.* Translated by Margaret Raine Hunt. Australia: The Planet, 2013. Kindle.

Guidry, Jeff. *An Eagle Named Freedom: My True Story of a Remarkable Friendship.* Toronto: HarperCollins, 2011. Kindle.

Halbertal, Moshe, and Avishai Margalit. *Idolatry.* Translated by Naomi Goldblum. Cambridge, MA: Harvard University Press, 1998.

Harjo, Joy. "Eagle Poem." In *Mad Love and War,* 65. Middletown, CT: Wesleyan University Press, 1990.

Haupt, Lyanda Lynn. *Crow Planet: Essential Wisdom from the Urban Wilderness.* New York: Back Bay, 2009.

Hearne, Vicki. *Adam's Task: Calling Animals by Name.* New York: Vintage, 1987.

Hedges Chris. *Empire of Illusion: The End of Literacy and the Triumph of Spectacle.* Toronto: Knopf Canada, 2009. Kindle.

Hedges, Chris, and Joe Sacco. *Days of Destruction, Days of Revolt.* Toronto: Knopf Canada, 2012. Kindle.

Hicks, Edward. *A Peaceable Season.* Introduction by Eleanore Price Mather. Princeton, NJ: Pyne, 1973.

Hillman, James. *Animal Presences.* Putnam, CT: Spring, 2008. Kindle.

Historical Society of Pennsylvania. "Wampum Belt." https://hsp.org/education/primary-sources/belt-of-wampum/.

Holland, Jennifer S. "Locusts Eat the Crops of Madagascar—and Each Other, Too." *KUAF National Public Radio,* September 3, 2014. https://www.kuaf.com/post/locusts-eat-crops-madagascar-and-each-other-too/.

Holtz, Shalom E. "Reading Biblical Law." In *The Jewish Study Bible,* 2nd ed., edited by Adele Berlin and Marc Zvi Brettler, 2201–7. Oxford: Oxford University Press, 2014.

Horowitz, Alexandra. *Inside of a Dog: What Dogs See, Smell, and Know.* New York: Scribner, 2009.

House, Tina."BC Elder Talks about Why Gathering of Eagles in Vancouver Should Concern Everyone." *APTN News,* February 9, 2017. https://www.aptnnews.ca/national-news/b-c-elder-talks-about-why-gathering-of-eagles-in-vancouver-should-concern-everyone/.

Husserl, Edmund. *Ideas: General Introduction to Pure Phenomenology.* Translated by W. R. Boyce Gibson. London: Routledge, 2012. Ebook. Originally published 1913.

"In the Spirit of the Donkey." Narrated by Jean Dalrymple. Tapestry. *CBC Radio,* April 2, 2015. https://www.cbc.ca/radio/tapestry/wine-wisdom-and-work-1.3018195/in-the-spirit-of-the-donkey-a-tapestry-donkumentary-1.3018239/.

Ivins, Molly, and Lou Dubose. *Bushwhacked: Life in George W. Bush's America.* New York: Random House, 2003. Kindle.

Jennings, Francis. *The Invasion of America: Indians, Colonialism, and the Cant of Conquest.* Chapel Hill, NC: Omohundro Institute and University of North Carolina Press, 2010.

JPS Hebrew-English Tanakh. 2nd ed. Philadelphia: Jewish Publication Society, 1999.

Juergensmeyer, Mark. *Terror in the Mind of God: The Global Rise of Religious Violence.* 4th ed. Oakland, CA: University of California Press, 2017. Kindle.

Kaufman, Mark. "How This Big Locust Plague Will End." *Mashable.com,* May 20, 2020. https://mashable.com/article/locust-plague-how-it-will-end/.

Kimmerer, Robin Wall. *Braiding Sweetgrass: Indigenous Wisdom, Scientific Knowledge and the Teachings of Plants.* Minneapolis: Milkweed Editions, 2013. Kindle.

Klein, Naomi. *This Changes Everything: Capitalism vs. the Climate.* Toronto: Knopf, 2014.

Klein, Seth. *A Good War: Mobilizing Canada for the Climate Emergency.* Toronto: ECW, 2020.

Korten, David. *When Corporations Rule the World.* 3rd ed. Oakland, CA: Berrett-Koehler, 2015. Kindle.

Kravitz, Leonard, and Kerry M. Olitzky, eds. *Pirkei Avot: A Modern Commentary on Jewish Ethics.* New York: UAHC, 1993.

Kugel, James L. *The Bible as It Was.* Cambridge: Belknap, 1997.

Leibowitz, Nechama. *New Studies in Shemot Exodus.* Translated by Aryeh Newman. Jerusalem: Maor Wallach, 1996.

———. *New Studies in Vayikra Leviticus,* vol. 1. Translated by Rafael Fisch and Avner Tomaschoff. Jerusalem: Eliner Library, 1993.

Lerner, Berel Dov. "Timid Grasshoppers and Fierce Locusts: An Ironic Pair of Biblical Metaphors." *Vetus Testamentum* 49.4 (1999) 545–48.

Lewis, Michael. *The Fifth Risk.* New York: Norton, 2018.

Lillywhite, Harvey B. *How Snakes Work: Structure, Function and Behavior of the World's Snakes.* Oxford: Oxford University Press, 2014.

Macdonald, Jake. "In the Company of Crows." *Canadian Geographic,* March 10, 2020. https://www.canadiangeographic.ca/article/company-crows/.

Maclaine, James. *Snakes.* Illustrated by Paul Parker and Becka Moor. London: Usborne, 2015.

Maimonides, Moses. *The Guide for the Perplexed.* Translated by M. Friedlander. 2nd ed. Wilmington, DE: Veritatis Splendor, 2013. Kindle. Originally published 1904.

Malbim, Meir Leibush ben Yehiel Michel. *Commentary on Daniel.* Sefaria. https://www.sefaria.org/Malbim_on_Daniel?lang=en/.

Margaliot, Reuven, ed. *Sefer Habahir and Tiquney Hazohar.* Jerusalem: Mossad Harav Kook, 1994.

Marzluff, John M. *In the Company of Crows and Ravens.* New Haven, CT: Yale University Press, 2007.

May, Gerald G. *The Wisdom of Wilderness.* New York: HarperCollins, 2006.

McLachlan, Stacey. "Where Do Those Crows Go Each Night?" *Vancouver Magazine,* December 29, 2017. https://www.vanmag.com/city-informer-where-crows-go-night.

McNally, Michael D. *Honouring Elders: Aging Authority and Ojibwe Religion.* New York: Columbia University Press, 2009.

Mechilta de Rabbi Shimon b. Jochai. Translated by D. Hoffman. Frankfurt: Kaufmann, 1905.

Messinger, Ruth W. "Rights and Responsibilities." *My Jewish Learning.* https://www.myjewishlearning.com/article/rights-amp-responsibilities/

Midrash Aggadah. Sefaria. https://www.sefaria.org/Midrash_Aggadah?lang=en.

Midrash Rabbah on Bereisheet. Jerusalem: Midrash Hamevuar Institute, 1984.

Mikraot Gedolot. Jerusalem: Hamaor, 1990.

Tanchuma. Translated and edited by Samuel L. Berman. Hoboken, NJ: Ktav, 1996. https://www.sefaria.org/Midrash_Tanchuma?lang=bi/.

Milgrom, Jacob. *Leviticus: A Continental Commentary.* Minneapolis: Augsburg Fortress, 2004.

———. *Leviticus 1–16: A New Translation and Commentary.* Anchor Bible. New York: Doubleday, 1991.

Miller, J. R. *Compact, Contract, Covenant: Aboriginal Treaty-Making in Canada.* Toronto: University of Toronto Press, 2009.

Morrison, Chanan. *Gold from the Land of Israel: A New Light on the Weekly Torah Portion from the Writings of Rabbi Abraham Isaac HaCohen Kook.* New York: Urim, 2006. Kindle.

Nachman of Breslov. *Likutey Moharan.* Jerusalem: Breslov Research Institute, 1995.

National Geographic. "Locusts." https://www.nationalgeographic.com/animals/invertebrates/group/locusts/.

Neusner, Jacob. *Introduction to Rabbinic Literature.* New Haven, CT: Yale University Press, 1999.

Newman, Andrew. "The Treaty of Shackamaxon." *The Encyclopedia of Greater Philadelphia.* https://philadelphiaencyclopedia.org/archive/treaty-of-shackamaxon-2/.

O'Leary, Jim. *Langara College Crow Trax: Crow Attack Tracker.* https://giscourses.net/crowtrax/crowtrax.html/.

Oreskes, Naomi, and Eric Conway. *Merchants of Doubt: How a Handful of Scientists Obscured the Truth on Issues from Tobacco Smoke to Global Warming.* London: Bloomsbury, 2010. Kindle.

Palmater, Pamela. "My Tribe, My Heirs and Their Heirs Forever: Living Mi'kmaw Treaties." In *Living Treaties: Narrating Mi'kmaw Treaty Relations,* edited by Marie Battiste. Sydney, NS: Cape Breton University Press, 2016. Kindle.

Paltiel, Yossi. "Kinesher Yair Kino" [As an eagle awakens its nest]. *Insidechassidus. org,* January 3, 2018. https://insidechassidus.org/kinesher-yair-kino-5746.

Pardes, Ilana. *Countertraditions in the Bible: A Feminist Approach.* Cambridge: Harvard University Press, 1992.

Patta, Raj Bharat. "Palm Sunday: A Celebration of Political Hegemony." *Political Theology,* April 7, 2017. https://politicaltheology.com/palm-sunday-a-celebration-of-counter-hegemony-raj-bharat-patta/.

Pierce, John D. "Review of Tool Use in Insects." *The Florida Entomologist* 69.1 (1986) 95–104.

Proudfoot, Richard, Ann Thompson, and David Scott Kastan, eds. *Shakespeare: Complete Works*. 2nd ed. London: Bloomsbury, 2011.

Pynn, Larry. "Ladner Landfill Becomes Bald Eagle Haven." *Vancouver Sun*, February 18, 2016. https://vancouversun.com/news/metro/ladner-landfill-becomes-bald-eagle-haven/.

Radak, David Kimchi. *Commentary on Isaiah*. Sefaria. https://www.sefaria.org/Radak_on_Isaiah?lang=en/.

Reid, Bill, and Robert Bringhurst. *The Raven Steals the Light*. Vancouver, BC: Douglas & McIntyre, 1988.

Ruddick, Sara. *Maternal Thinking: Towards a Politics of Peace*. Boston: Beacon, 1995.

Rush, Elizabeth. *Rising: Dispatches from the New American Shore*. Minneapolis: Milkweed, 2018.

Savage, Candace. *Bird Brains: The Intelligence of Crows, Ravens, Magpies, and Jays*. Vancouver, BC: Greystone, 2018.

Schaefer, Donovan O. *Religious Affects: Animality, Evolution and Power*. Chapel Hill, NC: Duke University Press, 2015.

Seidenberg, David. *Kabbalah and Ecology*. Cambridge: Cambridge University Press, 2015.

Selig, Jennifer Leigh. *Integration: The Psychology and Mythology of Martin Luther King, Jr. and His (Unfinished) Therapy with the Soul of America*. Carpinteria, CA: Mandorla, 2012.

Sherman, Nosson. *Perek Shira: The Song of the Universe*. New York: Artscroll, 2004.

Simkins, Ronald A. "God, History, and the Natural World in the Book of Joel." *The Catholic Biblical Quarterly* 55 (1993) 435–52.

Simmons, Paula, and Carol Ekarius. *Storey's Guide to Raising Sheep*. 5th ed. North Adams, MA: Storey, 2019.

Slifkin, Natan. *Perek Shira: Nature's Song*. Jerusalem: Zoo Torah, 2011.

Sprowles, Michael R. "Mine Mules: Their Use in Coal Mines in the United States." *Mining History Journal* 18 (2011) 26–32.

Stone, Ken. *Reading the Hebrew Bible with Animal Studies*. Stanford, CA: Stanford University Press, 2018. Kindle.

Steen, David A. *Secrets of Snakes: The Science beyond the Myths*. College Station, TX: Texas A & M University Press, 2019.

Steinsaltz, Adin. *The Thirteen Petalled Rose*. Jerusalem: Maggid, 1996. Kindle.

Swift, Kaeli. "In the Company of Corvids." Workshop, North Cascades Environmental Institute, July 26–28, 2019.

Tekiela, Stan. *Majestic Eagles: Compelling Facts and Images of the Bald Eagle*. Cambridge, MN: Adventure, 2007.

Thomas, Elizabeth Marshall. *The Hidden Life of Deer*. New York: HarperCollins, 2009.

———. *The Hidden Life of Dogs*. Boston: Mariner, 2010.

————. *The Tribe of Tiger: Cats and Their Culture.* New York: Gallery, 2001.

Thomson, Aly Thomson. "Ancient Fish Species Discovered in Nova Scotia Opens Door for Future Research." *Canoe.com*, May 26 2018. https://canoe.com/news/national/ancient-fish-species-discovered-in-nova-scotia-opens-door-for-future-research/.

Tristram, Henry Baker. *The Natural History of the Bible.* 1867. Reprint, Miami: HardPress, 2017. Kindle.

Turtle Valley Donkey Refuge. https://turtlevalleydonkeyrefuge.com/.

Viviers, H. "The 'Wonderful' Donkey—Of Real and Fabled Donkeys." *Theological Studies* 75.3 (2019) 1–8.

Wallace, Naomi. Interview. September 10, 2020.

Way, Kenneth C. "Animals in the Prophetic World: Literary Reflections on Numbers 22 and 1 Kings 13." *Journal for the Study of the Old Testament* 34.1 (2009) 47–62.

White, E. B. *Charlotte's Web.* Reprint, New York: Barnes and Noble, 1997.

Wicken, William. "Fact Sheet on Peace and Friendship Treaties in the Maritimes and Gaspé." Government of Canada, September 15, 2010. https://www.rcaanc-cirnac.gc.ca/eng/1100100028599/1539609517566.

William Davidson Talmud. *Sefaria.* 2015. https://www.sefaria.org/texts/Talmud/.

Wilson, E. O. *The Creation: An Appeal to Save Life on Earth.* New York: Norton, 2006.

Winston, Mark. *Bee Time: Lessons from the Hive.* Cambridge: Harvard University Press, 2014.

Wirzba, Norman. *Food and Faith: A Theology of Eating.* Cambridge: Cambridge University Press, 2011.

————. *The Paradise of God: Renewing Religion in an Ecological Age.* Oxford: Oxford University Press, 2008.

Wittgenstein, Ludwig. *Philosophical Investigations.* Translated by G. E. M. Anscombe, P. M. S. Hacker, and Joachim Schulte. 4th ed. Hoboken, NJ: Wiley-Blackwell, 2010.

Wolak, Arthur J. "Alcohol and the Fate of Nadab and Abihu: A Biblical Cautionary Tale against Inebriation." *Jewish Bible Quarterly* 41.4 (2013) 219–26.

Yamauchi, Edwin M. "Ancient Ecologies and the Biblical Perspective." *Journal of the American Scientific Affiliation* 32.4 (1980) 193–202.

Zamora, Lois Parkinson, and Wendy B. Faris, eds. *Magical Realism: Theory, History, Community.* Durham, NC: Duke University Press, 1995. Kindle.